GREAT RECORD LABELS

GREAT RECORD LABELS

AL CIMINO

THE
APPLE
PRESS

A QUINTET BOOK

Published by The Apple Press
6 Blundell Street
London N7 9BH

ISBN 1-85076-416-6

This book was designed and produced by
Quintet Publishing Limited
6 Blundell Street
London N7 9BH

Creative Director: Richard Dewing
Designer: Stuart Walden
Project Editor: Damian Thompson
Editor: Robert Stewart
Picture Researcher: Mirco De Cet
Photographer: Ali Solawala

Typeset in Great Britain by
Central Southern Typesetters, Eastbourne
Manufactured in Singapore by
Eray Scan (Pte) Ltd.
Printed in Singapore by
Star Standard Industries Private Ltd.

CONTENTS

Introduction 6

THE FIFTIES 8

Sun 10

Chess 17

Atlantic 21

RCA 24

THE SIXTIES 28

Stax 30

Motown 38

Decca 47

EMI 52

Capitol 57

Apple 62

A&M 66

THE SEVENTIES 68

CBS 70

Warner Brothers 76

Elektra/Asylum and the Dave Geffen Label 79

Island 82

Stiff 86

THE EIGHTIES 88

Polygram 90

MCA 94

Virgin 98

ZTT 102

THE NINETIES 104

Def Jam 106

Four Decades of Essential Records 109

Index 110

Picture Credits 112

 # INTRODUCTION

The production, manufacture, marketing and distribution of records is the art that conceals. Although the major labels have their huge corporate headquarters — CBS's Black Rock, Capitol's Capitol Tower — little is known of what goes on inside. The labels hide behind the artists who lend the industry its glamour. In fact, according to music business consultant, Barry McKay, the labels don't care much about the artists at all. "Artists, they are the scum, the product," he says. "They come, they go." It is the record labels that go on forever.

Many artists complain that they are promoted as if they were soap powder. Rolling Stones guitarist, Keith Richards, once said: "Decca are supposed to be making records; they might as just as easily be making baked beans. A record to them is just a piece of plastic, and what's on there doesn't really matter. I'd rather the Mafia than Decca."

The old time music publisher, Eddie Kassner, summed up the music industry even more succinctly. "They're all fucking animals," he said.

The rip-offs are legendary. The world is full of artists who had a hit record and never saw a cent in return. Little Richard once complained: "Many companies have not paid me yet. They tore my toes and my fingers. I didn't have nothing to crawl with. I'm amazed. All these hit records. Everyone done sung them but my grandmama. And everyone was rich but me."

Alan Klein started his career in management when he ran a practised eye over Bobby Darin's books and found $100,000 outstanding. Klein went on to perform the same trick for the Rolling Stones and the Beatles. Tom Petty was driven into bankruptcy when his record sales did not match up to the tour expenses that his record company were charging him. Florence Ballard, founder member of the Supremes, died penniless on welfare after being pushed out by Motown. The former Beatles, The Who, Wham! and many others have spent thousands in litigation over royalties. But, as Morris Levy, owner of Roulette Records and other labels, used to tell his artists: "Royalty? If you want royalty, go to England."

The industry is studded with fabled characters. CBS president, Walter Yetnikoff, is known for his temper tantrums and invective. MCA's Irving Azoff is widely respected as a son-of-a-bitch. And there are some choice stories about the industry's Mr Nice Guy, Richard Branson. Branson, no stranger to the courtrooms in disputes with his own artists, issued a writ against Stiff Records's Dave Robinson after they played a round of golf together. Rattled after taking nine shots on the fourteenth hole, Branson brought up an ancient dispute they'd had over an artist's contract.

Yet, despite their shortcomings, the record labels have acted as catalysts in the growth of rock and pop. They have plucked obscure acts from remote parts of the United States and England and put them on an international stage. Without Sun and Chess there would be no rock and roll. Without Stax and Motown there would be no soul. Without Def Jam rap would never have happened. And without Atlantic . . . well it doesn't bear thinking about.

So, despite the hype, the rip-offs, the inflated egos, the unethical business deals, the fickle fads and the massive profit margins, the record-buying public probably owes the great record labels as much of a debt as the labels owe their artists in unpaid royalties.

RIGHT: **Tin Pan Alley was 28th Street in Manhattan. Up until the late fifties, songwriters, small music publishers and song pluggers worked within a rabbit warren of small offices around this famous street. London's equivalent was Denmark Street in the West End.**

THE FIFTIES

The record industry had been established for over 50 years by the time that rock and roll came along. The major record labels were entrenched. In the United States, there were CBS and RCA Victor; in Great Britain, EMI and Decca; and in continental Europe, Polydor. But across the United States there were also hundreds of smaller labels, recording jazz, country and western, folk music and rhythm and blues.

Most of the R&B labels that spawned the rock-and-roll revolution were owned by whites who ruthlessly exploited the black talent that recorded with them. One of the legendary figures of the 1950s was Morris Levy, owner of Roulette Records and many others. Like many of the promoters, managers and record label heads of his day, he paid his artists late, or not at all.

CADILLACS FOR ROYALTIES

Others, like Hy Weiss, founder of the Old Town label, would fob an artist off with a Cadillac. Surprisingly many were happy with a new car, rather than the hundreds of thousands of dollars they were owed. This practice did not trouble Weiss's conscience. After all, he reasoned, the artists were nothing more than "bums off the street". A little glory and the best girls on the block should be enough. Besides, he had other things to spend his money on – payola. Weiss was reputedly the inventor of the $50 handshake. DJs would get a crisp $50 bill to play his records.

The quintessential 1950s label-owner, Morris Levy, had a long career in the music industry. During the late 1940s and early 1950s, Levy ran clubs, including the world-famous jazz venue, Birdland, named for the famous jazz saxophonist, Charlie Parker. But he spotted the secret of fortune — if not fame — in the music industry early on: the real money came from owning copyright. Clubs open and close. Artists come and go. Records climb the charts and fall again. But copyright lasts (almost) forever.

Levy's first publishing copyright was on "Lullaby of Birdland", which he commissioned for his nightclub. It became a jazz classic. "The Yellow Rose of Texas" came later. It is played in the United States only slightly less often than "Happy Birthday to You". Each time it is played it earns a few pennies, and those pennies soon mount up.

MORRIS LEVY AND ALAN FREED

In 1956 Levy started a record label of his own, Roulette. Within five weeks he had a number one hit with Buddy Knox and a number 11 with Jimmy Bowen. Levy later joined forces with Alan Freed, the DJ who, more than anyone else, was responsible for the rock-and-roll explosion of the late 1950s.

Freed fell from grace during the 1960 payola scandal. What brought him down was plugging Chuck Berry's first hit, "Maybellene", to which Chess Records had let him add his name as co-writer, thus earning him royalties. An indictment ended his career.

Levy remained untouched by the scandal, though he shamelessly added his own name to Frankie Lymon's as co-author of "Why Do Fools Fall in Love?" and other Lymon songs. When sued for the royalties he had skimmed off, Levy explained that, though he did not actually write songs "like Chopin", he would get together with Lymon, "get a beat going and put the music and words together".

Unlike most label bosses, who are more often than not lawyers these days, Levy did not use the courts to get his way. He preferred direct action. He is reputed to have broken up a pressing-plant, which he believed to be bootlegging his records, with a baseball bat.

It was in the world of Levy and Weiss that a naive young label-owner in Memphis, Tennessee, launched the rock-and-roll revolution. Sam Phillips had been recording black artists on his Sun label, often licensing them to Chess, for about two years when he came to the conclusion that, if he could only find a white artist who could sing like a black, he could make "a million dollars". He found Elvis Presley.

RIGHT: **During the fifties, the juke box was a major medium for plugging records. Stacking juke boxes gave organized crime its first foothold in the music business.**

SUN

Rock and roll began at the Sun Studios in Memphis — not in August, 1954, with the discovery of the young Elvis Presley, but in June, 1951, when Jackie Brenston recorded his hit "Rocket 88" there. The studio — a converted radiator shop at 706 Union Avenue, Memphis — had been built in 1950 by Sam Phillips, a DJ and fully trained radio engineer from the local station WRAC Memphis. It was so small that business meetings had to take place in Miss Taylor's Restaurant next door — "third booth from the window".

Phillips's Memphis Recording Service touted for business. The sign that hung outside his storefront read: "We record anything — anywhere — any time." Phillips soon realized that there was a market for local black rhythm-and-blues artists. Phillips had had a long-term love affair with R&B. Brought up on a farm in Florence, Alabama, he had been introduced to the blues and black field hollers by a blind sharecropper called Silas Payne, whom he knew as "Uncle" and had hung out in the blues clubs on Memphis's famous Beale Street, crossing the race line at a time when segregation still ruled in the South.

The death of his father allowed Phillips to abandon a planned career as a lawyer and become a teenage disc jockey at WLAY in Muscle Shoals. He moved on to WLAC in Nashville and then, in 1944, to WRAC in Memphis.

Spotting the Trends

In the early 1950s, with the young Ike Turner as his talent scout and leader of the studio's backing band, Phillips recorded Chester "Howlin' Wolf" Burnett, B.B. King, Junior Parker, Bobby "Blue" Bland, Walter Horton, Earl Hooker, Rosco Gordon and Johnny Ace. He leased these sides to Chess in Chicago and RPM in Los Angeles and to other R&B labels like Duke and Modern. Then came Brenston's "Rocket 88".

Phillips was quick to spot a trend and in December, 1951, he introduced his own label, Sun. Sun's first hit was the raw, rowdy "Bear Cat" by Rufus Thomas. Other recordings came from Junior Parker,

TOP: **Jerry Lee Lewis failed to reveal his talent in his first audition tape for producer "Cowboy Jack" Clements at Sun Records in 1956. But owner Sam Phillips called him back to cover country and western hit "Crazy Arms". It became a regional hit.**

ABOVE: **At Sun, Sam Phillips brought together the strands of black and white music, of the blues and country and western, and, in the process, created rock and roll.**

"ROCKET 88"

Jackie Brenston was playing sax in Ike Turner's band, the Kings of Rhythm, when he wrote this classic — a jumping car song with honking sax and a steam-train rhythm. Sam Phillips recorded it with a new technique later described as "documentary". The sound was spare, with a simple tape echo to project the singer. Leased to Chess, the record reached number one in the R&B charts in 1951. It was Brenston's one and only hit. Phillips had bought the song for $900 and sold the rights to a country-and-western singer called Bill Haley, who used it to begin a new career in rock and roll.

ABOVE: **Sun Records' other king —
B. B. King. His first hits on the
RPM label were recorded at the
Sun studios in Memphis in the
early 1950s.**

RIGHT: **The pumping piano and
manic voice of Jerry Lee Lewis
helped to continue the success of
Sun Records' distinctive sunrise
label, after Elvis Presley had
moved on to RCA.**

SUN

Justis Music,
Inc.
BMI

U-336
Vocal
2:37

IT HURT ME SO
(Rich-Justis)
JERRY LEE LEWIS
AND HIS PUMPING PIANO
312
MEMPHIS, TENNESSEE

SUN

SUN

RIGHT: **Rufus Thomas gave the Sun label its first hit with "Bear Cat" in 1953. He and his daughter Carla, the self-styled "world's oldest teenager", also helped to establish another label—Stax.**

LEFT: **Although Elvis Presley moved from Memphis label Sun to New York-based RCA in 1955, he never moved out of Memphis. He is seen here checking the competition in a local Memphis record store in 1957.**

Billy "the Kid" Emerson, the Prisonaires (from Tennessee State Penitentiary), Isaiah "Dr" Ross and Jimmy DeBerry.

By 1954 other labels specializing in black music had sprung up – like Checker, Atlantic and Specialty. Phillips needed his white man who could sing like a black and in August, 1954, Elvis Presley walked into the Memphis Recording Service to record a song, "My Happiness", to his mother as a birthday present. Phillips liked what he heard. He got Presley to record a demo and, later, signed him.

Presley tried to record some country ballads with the session musicians, Scotty Moore and Bill Black, but Phillips was disappointed. It was only when Presley tried a blues song, with another Sun artist, Arthur "Big Boys" Crudup, that he hit pay dirt. The song was "That's All Right, Mama". A local DJ, Dewey Phillips, picked up on it and gave it airtime – and the rest is history.

In 18 months Phillips recorded five hit singles, mainly cover versions of black songs. But, not being a Morris Levy, he did not make his million. Instead, in 1955 he sold Presley's contract to RCA Victor for just $35,000, plus a $5,000 signing bonus. Nor did Phillips keep the rights to any of the songs that Presley recorded. He played it straight. For Elvis's early work both he and the writer got paid.

Presley's new manager was "Colonel" Tom Parker, an illegal Dutch immigrant and former carnival barker. His name appeared as co-author on the songs that Presley recorded for RCA and he took his cut of the royalties. Five years after Presley's death in 1977, the courts ruled that Parker had helped himself to money rather more generously than the contracts stipulated.

Phillips used the money from the sale of Presley's contract to develop new white talent, turning the Sun label into the hothouse of

SUN

ABOVE: **Carl Perkins gave the Sun label its first national hit with "Blue Suede Shoes". It made number two in the 1956 pop charts. Elvis Presley's cover version (an EP in the US) only made number 20 in America, but climbed to number nine in the UK.**

rock and roll. His new signings included Carl Perkins, Jerry Lee Lewis, Charlie Rich, Johnny Cash, Roy Orbison, Carl Smith and Billy Lee Riley. The label's most commercially successful recordings were Carl Perkins's "Blue Suede Shoes", which sold a million, Johnny Cash's "I Walk the Line" and Jerry Lee Lewis's "Whole Lotta Shakin' Goin' On".

Phillips had lit the fuse of the rock explosion, but the talent he had discovered soon moved on. By 1968 Sun had ceased operations and in 1969 Phillips sold the label – and its priceless archives – to Shelby Singleton. With the money from that sale – shrewdly invested in broadcasting, hotels and mining – Phillips eventually made his million.

Sun reissued material through Singleton's SSS International and the Sun Studios continued to record. The Amazing Rhythm Aces produced several albums there. Phillips has also continued to dabble. He produced two tracks of John Prine's *Pink Cadillac* album in 1979 and his two sons produced the rest.

Sun reissues are now handled by SSS in the United States and Charly in Great Britain.

LEFT: **Country-and-western singer Carl Smith was part of Sam Phillips' second wave of signings, but failed to make the cross-over into rock and roll.**

RIGHT: **On a Sun tour with Carl Perkins and Johnny Cash, the shy Jerry Lee Lewis was told to "make a fuss". Next night he stood up and kicked the piano stool over – "the Killer" was born.**

SUN

CHESS

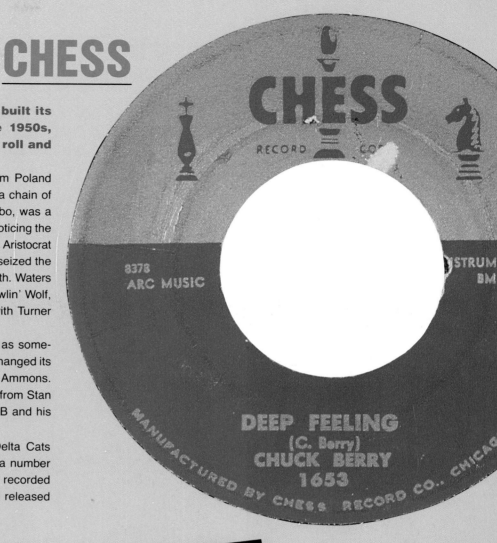

he Chess label began with the blues. It built its reputation on rhythm and blues in the 1950s, became a driving force behind rock and roll and finally moved into soul.

Leonard and Phil Chess were Jewish immigrants from Poland who settled in Chicago in 1928. By the 1940s they owned a chain of taverns on Chicago's Southside. One of them, the Mocambo, was a venue for jazzmen like Billy Eckstine. The Chess brothers, noticing the lack of recording facilities for black acts, bought into the focal Aristocrat label in 1947. When Muddy Waters came to Aristocrat they seized the opportunity to capture and preserve the sound of the old South. Waters attracted other R&B artists and Ike Turner brought them Howlin' Wolf, whom he had first recorded on a field trip of Arkansas – with Turner himself on piano and James Cotton on blues harp.

Leonard and Phil Chess immediately recognized Wolf as something new. In 1950 they bought out the Aristocrat label and changed its name to Chess. The first single they released was by Gene Ammons. He had played tenor sax with Billy Eckstine and taken over from Stan Getz in the Woody Herman band. Then he veered into R&B and his "This Foolish Heart" made the R&B top ten.

Elmore James, Gordon Rosco and Ike Turner and Delta Cats were other early Chess signings. Turner brought the label a number one R&B hit when his early group, the Kings of Rhythm, recorded "Rocket 88" at Sun Studios. It was licensed by Chess and released under the name of the vocalist, Jackie Brenston.

TOP RIGHT: **The colour of the Chess label shows its blues origins. The Chess pieces speak for themselves, though Phil and Leonard never revealed who was the knight and who the bishop.**

RIGHT: **Chuck Berry moved Chess on from its blues and R&B origins and turned it into one of the foremost rock-and-roll labels with a succession of his early classics.**

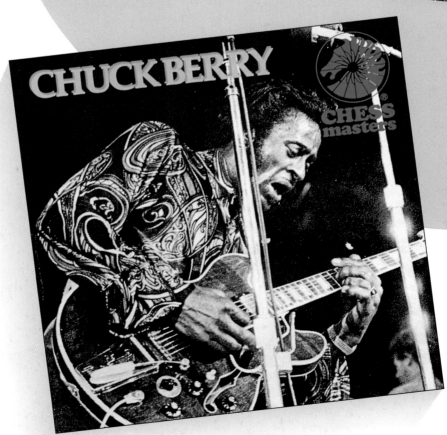

LEFT: **The legendary blues singer Muddy Waters was with the Aristocrat label when the Chess brothers took over. Waters left Chess in 1973 and sued the company for back royalties.**

Chess took on Willie Dixon as producer, arranger, session bassist and, so Leonard Chess described him, "right-hand man". Dixon went on to write "I Just Want to Make Love to You" and "Little Red Rooster", which the Rolling Stones later recorded.

In 1953 the Chess brothers started the Checker label to handle the gospel sound of Little Milton, Little Walter, the Flamingos and Lowell Fulson.

Berry makes the cross-over

By the mid-1950s Chess was leading the pack in rock and roll. A young guitarist called Chuck Berry, who had come to them as a session musician, persuaded Muddy Waters to let him sit in on a session. Berry's guitar technique and fluent style impressed Waters. Chess signed him and quickly released "Maybellene", with "Wee Wee Hours" – which Berry preferred – on the B side.

Alan Freed took an interest in "Maybellene" and in exchange for his suggestions on how to make it more commercial took a co-credit. Freed gave it the airplay that carried it into the top ten. The record took Chess into the cross-over market – black songs that made it into the white charts – and launched Berry's long career.

Bo Diddley and Dale Hawkins, on the Checker label, also crossed over into the pop charts in the late 1950s, while the Dells, Etta James,

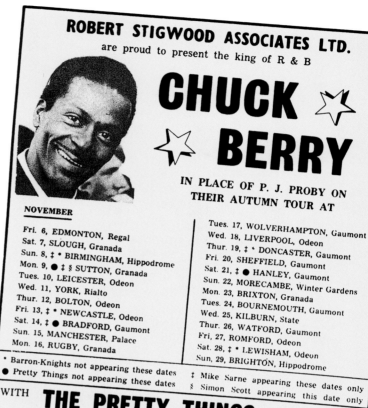

ROBERT STIGWOOD ASSOCIATES LTD.
are proud to present the king of R & B

CHUCK ★ ★ BERRY

IN PLACE OF P. J. PROBY ON THEIR AUTUMN TOUR AT

NOVEMBER

Fri. 6, EDMONTON, Regal
Sat. 7, SLOUGH, Granada
Sun. 8, ‡ • BIRMINGHAM, Hippodrome
Mon. 9, • ‡ § SUTTON, Granada
Tues. 10, LEICESTER, Odeon
Wed. 11, YORK, Rialto
Thur. 12, BOLTON, Odeon
Fri. 13, ‡ • NEWCASTLE, Odeon
Sat. 14, ‡ • BRADFORD, Gaumont
Sun. 15, MANCHESTER, Palace
Mon. 16, RUGBY, Granada

Tues. 17, WOLVERHAMPTON, Gaumont
Wed. 18, LIVERPOOL, Odeon
Thur. 19, ‡ • DONCASTER, Gaumont
Fri. 20, SHEFFIELD, Gaumont
Sat. 21, ‡ • HANLEY, Gaumont
Sun. 22, MORECAMBE, Winter Gardens
Mon. 23, BRIXTON, Granada
Tues. 24, BOURNEMOUTH, Gaumont
Wed. 25, KILBURN, State
Thur. 26, WATFORD, Gaumont
Fri. 27, ROMFORD, Odeon
Sat. 28, ‡ • LEWISHAM, Odeon
Sun. 29, BRIGHTON, Hippodrome

• Barron-Knights not appearing these dates
● Pretty Things not appearing these dates
‡ Mike Sarne appearing these dates only
§ Simon Scott appearing this date only

WITH **THE PRETTY THINGS**

KIM WESTON and the EARL VAN DYKE QUARTET | THE TEA TIME FOUR | THE LE ROYS DON SPENCER

THE BARRON-KNIGHTS

ON SPECIFIED DATES

MIKE SARNE   **SIMON SCOTT**

RIGHT: **Chess was always popular in Britain. It was a source of many of the songs covered by English bands in the early sixties. But English fans got their chance to see the real thing when Chuck Berry toured the UK in November 1964.**

LEFT **Chuck Berry's back catalogue provided much of the material that fuelled the British invasion of the sixties. And many even imitated his famous "duck walk".**

the Monotones and Clarence "Frogman" Henry gave the label a strong presence in both the rock and soul markets. Meanwhile the Chess brothers slimmed down their blues stable to the classic line-up of Muddy Waters, Howlin' Wolf, Sonny Boy Williamson, Otis Rush and Buddy Guy.

At the beginning of the 1960s they had Koko Taylor, Sugar Pie Desanto and Fontella Bass on their lists. But the Chess label was in decline. Shortly before the death of Leonard Chess in 1969, it was sold to General Recording Tape, one of the two giant tape manufacturers in the United States.

GRT moved the Chess offices to New York. Leonard's son, Marshall Chess, stayed on with GRT for a short time, but they deleted most of Chess's blues and rock-and-roll artists from their lists and tried to push the rhythm and blues acts into an association with their established Janus label.

When the Rolling Stones decided to break with Decca and London and start their own label, they looked for an American distributor. Their first choice would have been Chess – many of the Stones's early songs had been Chess covers. But Chess was no longer the company the Rolling Stones once knew and loved. So they signed a distribution deal with Atlantic. They managed, however, to persuade Marshall Chess to come in with them as their American label manager.

The Chess list ended up with MCA, who handle re-issues.

CHESS

ABOVE: **Clarence "Frogman" Henry had his first hit on the Argo label with "Ain't Got No Home". The novelty R&B hit gave him his nickname — he put on a funny voice and sang "like a frog".**

LEFT: **Bo Diddley had a string of hits on Chess's sister label Checker. He made the label famous and stuck with Checker throughout his long career.**

19

CHESS

ATLANTIC

Ahmet Ertegun was the man behind Atlantic Records. He was the son of the Turkish ambassador to the United States and was studying at Georgetown University in Washington when he was first taken with jazz. He persuaded a friend, Herb Abaramson, to record some of the black jazz bands they had heard in the neighbourhood clubs and with a third, silent investor – a Turkish dentist, Dr Sabit – they formed a label and moved to New York.

In October, 1947, they were grabbing every black act they could find. Early signings included Erroll Garner and Tiny Grimes, but Atlantic's first hit was Stick McGhee's R&B classic, "Drinkin' Wine Spo-Dee-O-Dee". It sold 400,000 copies and made number three in what *Billboard* still called their "race music" chart. R&B plainly was the way to go.

Atlantic recorded Joe Turner, Ray Charles, Little Esther, Chuck Willis and LaVern Baker. But their new artists were too hard-edged to make much impression on the pop charts and the company brought in ex-*Billboard* R&B reviewer, Jerry Wexler, to sort out the problem. He softened the edge of R&B and made it palatable for a white audience. Wexler put the unknown lead singer of the Dominoes, Clyde McPhatter,

OPPOSITE: **Buddy Guy was a house musician at Chess and had his own hit for the label with "Stone Crazy", which reached number twelve in the R&B charts in 1962. In 1968, he moved on to Atlantic with Junior Wells.**

LEFT: **Ahmet Ertegun, chairman and founder of Atlantic Records, is multilingual. He can speak English, Turkish, French and perfect black jive.**

ABOVE: **Wilson Pickett, one of the great soul singers, signed to Atlantic in 1963. After two flops, Jerry Wexler sent him south to Stax in Memphis to record with Booker T. and the MGs. The result was the classic "In the Midnight Hour", a number one R&B hit in 1965.**

BELOW: **Ray Charles invented "soul" on the Atlantic label in the mid-fifties by mixing the raunchy feel of rhythm and blues with the uplifting sound of gospel.**

LEFT: **Atlantic started as a jazz label. Jazz pianist Erroll Garner – a sideman of jazz legend Charlie "Bird" Parker – was one of the label's first signings.**

BELOW: **Big Joe Turner's R&B hit "Shake, Rattle and Roll" was written by fellow Atlantic star Ray Charles and boasted backing vocals by Atlantic bosses Ahmet Ertegun and Jerry Wexler. It was later covered by Bill Haley and Elvis Presley.**

with the Drifters – Atlantic's first crucial cross-over group. Wexler also brought in the famous songwriting team, Leiber and Stoller. They gave the string of cross-over hits to the Coasters. Atlantic also had a white star on their hands – Bobby Darin, who recorded on their Atco label.

Ertegun's brother, Neshui, a lecturer in folk music and jazz at UCLA, was recruited to handle the jazz roster, which included such progressive greats as the Modern Jazz Quartet, Charles Mingus and John Coltrane.

In 1960 Atlantic signed a distribution deal with Stax and, by using their studios in Memphis and also the Fame Studios in Muscle Shoals, Alabama, put themselves in touch with a lot of new, young soul talent. Their soul roster soon included Joe Tex, Percy Sledge, Sam and Dave, Otis Redding and Solomon Burke.

Atlantic did not, however, confine their attention to black talent. They signed white acts like Iron Butterfly, Buffalo Springfield, the Rascals, Crosby Stills Nash and Young, Led Zeppelin, Emerson Lake and Palmer, Yes, Eric Clapton and, in 1970, the Rolling Stones.

By the mid-1960s this mix of black and white, soul and rock, had transformed Atlantic from a specialist label into a major recording company. It was taken over by Warner Communications and in 1968 it became part of WEA (Warner Elektra Atlantic). Absorption by WEA did not inhibit Atlantic's independent style. The label continued to have success with Manhattan Transfer, Sister Sledge, Chic, Roberta Flack and Bette Midler.

RIGHT **Soul legend Wilson Pickett moved from his natural home on the Stax-Atlantic circuit to RCA records in 1973, then signed to EMI America in the early eighties.**

BOTTOM: **Atlantic continued its jazz tradition by signing the Modern Jazz Quartet to its jazz division, which was established in 1956.**

BELOW: **Jazz singer LaVern Baker turned to rhythm and blues when she signed to Atlantic. Between 1955 and 1965, she produced fifteen R&B hits with eight reaching the top ten.**

RCA

RCA was started by the American industrial giant, General Electric, in 1919. GE had invested $14 million in the British Marconi Company who, it believed, had the most practical radio broadcasting system for the United States.

The United States government wanted to keep control of broadcasting, but Congress backed the public's right to the airwaves under the First Amendment. GE founded the Radio Corporation of America in Delaware and within three years had sold one million radio sets at $75 a piece.

The Depression hit the recording industry hard: records were a luxury that people could ill afford. But the demand for radios continued since, after the initial outlay of $75, the entertainment they provided was free. In 1929 RCA bought the Victor Talking Machine Company, established in 1901 by Emile Berliner, the inventor of the gramophone.

ASCAP battles for royalties

RCA did not want Victor to produce records. They wanted its factories to make more radios. However, taking over Victor brought RCA an

OPPOSITE: **The Original Dixieland Jazz Band, the first white exponents of the new music, recorded on a number of labels. But all their hits – except one on Columbia – were recorded for the Victor label.**

TOP: **Actor Harry Belafonte began his singing career in the Broadway musical *Carmen Jones*. He was signed to the RCA label in 1955, after a 22-week gig as a folk singer in the Greenwich Village folk club, the Village Vanguard. His first hit for RCA was "Scarlet Ribbons".**

ABOVE: **Pat Boone had a string of 54 hits for Dot Records, a label for which RCA made an unsuccessful bid. The acceptable face of rock and roll – to parents at least – the clean-living crooner claimed to be a direct descendant of frontiersman Daniel Boone, but was certainly a direct rival to RCA's Elvis. He first found success as a country singer with Nashville's Republic Records, before signing to Dot in 1955.**

RIGHT: **RCA Victor celebrate the pressing of their billionth disc in suitably patriotic style. The record was "Stars and Stripes" by the Boston Symphony Orchestra.**

unexpected benefit when a battle broke out between ASCAP – the American Society of Composers, Authors and Publishers – and the radio companies. ASCAP wanted royalties each time a record was played on the air, while the stations believed that they bought the broadcast rights when they bought the record. ASCAP tried to ban the broadcast of the records of any of the other companies they represented. Suddenly, RCA found Victor's backlist – which included the earliest jazz records by the Original Dixieland Jazz Band, Al Jolson and Fats Waller – invaluable. And quickly they formed their RCA Victor music division to produce new music from Victor's recording and pressing facilities.

During the Swing era, RCA Victor recorded Benny Goodman, Glenn Miller, Duke Ellington and Tommy Dorsey with Frank Sinatra. Later the company went progressive with Dizzy Gillespie.

RIGHT: **When RCA bought Victor in 1929, they also bought Nipper the dog – or the use of him in the US, at least. Later, in 1955, they bought that other icon of pop culture, Elvis Presley.**

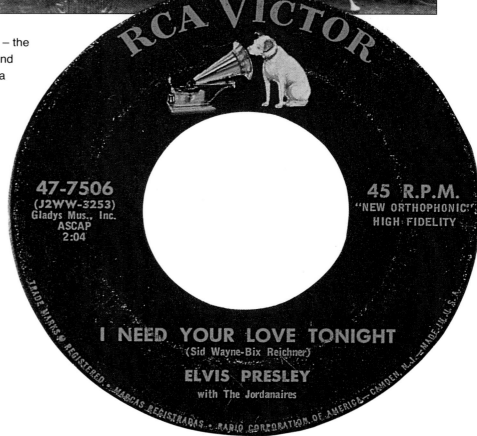

DAVID JACKSON

ABOVE: **The legendary be-bop star and innovator, Dizzy Gillespie, with his trademark upturned trumpet, was with RCA Victor in the late forties, before unsuccessfully setting up his own label in Detroit. He subsequently played under the Verve, Elektra and Pablo umbrellas.**

RIGHT: **Fats Waller was another of the big jazz stars that RCA found it had bought along with Victor. But his last recordings were on the US Army-sponsored V label, during the Musicians Union's strike in 1943. One of the recordings that were supposed to boost wartime morale was "The Reefer Song", which begins: "Dream about a reefer five foot long . . ."**

RCA Victor goes popular

In the late 1940s RCA Victor moved into pop with Perry Como and Dinah Shore. Then, in 1955, it won the race to buy Elvis Presley from Sam Phillips at Sun. Decca offered $5,000. The small, independent Dot Records offered $7,500. Atlantic had offered $25,000.

RCA signed Elvis Presley for just $35,000 – to Sam Phillips at Sun – and $5,000, split 75-25 by Elvis and his new manager, "Colonel" Tom Parker. Elvis also got a Cadillac Convertible as a "bonus" from RCA, who could afford to be generous because Presley really cost the company only a little over $10,000. They offset $15,000 in a deal with the music publishers, Hill and Range, who had exclusive rights to Presley's material. Hill and Range employees – who included Jerry Leiber and Mike Stoller – wrote the songs that Presley recorded, but Presley got his name on the records as co-writer, giving him a 50 per cent kickback.

During the 1960s RCA was quiescent. In the 1970s and 1980s it made a slight comeback with John Denver, Rick Springfield, Hall & Oates and Dolly Parton. And from Great Britain it signed the Sweet, David Bowie and the Eurythmics. Even so, RCA found itself slipping to the bottom of the league of majors.

In an attempt to halt the slide, RCA tried to take over Arista, the former Bell label, which had had successes with David Cassidy, Gary Glitter and the Bay City Rollers. Arista was run by the former CBS boss, Clive Davis, who had Barry Manilow and Whitney Houston on his lists. The company was jointly owned by Columbia Pictures and Bertelsmann Music Group, the German recording giant. And when the negotiations came to an end, RCA, instead of taking over Arista, found itself absorbed by Bertelsmann.

TOP RIGHT: **Elvis Presley on tour in 1955, the year RCA signed him. This is how the US Post Office have decided to commemorate Elvis on their stamps.** INSET: **Elvis survived the British invasion by becoming a crooner. He stayed with RCA for the remainder of his 22-year career.**

LAUNCHING THE LP

It was RCA Victor who first tried to launch the LP. In 1931 they doubled the number of grooves and changed the speed from the old 78 revolutions per minute to 33⅓ rpm. But the launch was a failure. The recordings were inferior and the pressings wore badly under the heavy pickups of that era. Resistance from the other record companies was strong and the market was depressed.

In 1927, 104 million records had been sold in the United States. By 1932 the economic slump had pushed the figure down to six million. RCA dropped its bold experiment. As a final humiliation, the company found that it had to go along with Columbia's LP system, launched in 1948.

ABOVE: **Glen Miller (centre) and his orchestra, like many RCA acts, would have benefited if the company had succeeded in their early launch of the LP. He had to record on 78s throughout his sadly curtailed career.**

THE SIXTIES

The major labels were slow to jump on the rock bandwagon. RCA went into the 1960s with Elvis Presley. But Capitol had lost Gene Vincent in 1959, when he emigrated to England. Bob Dylan was signed by CBS in 1961, but he was not exactly a rock act. He was signed as a folk singer by Columbia's legendary A&R man, John Hammond, who had discovered Billie Holiday in a Harlem speakeasy in 1933 and was to audition Bruce Springsteen. In between he had brought Count Basie, Aretha Franklin and George Benson to CBS. But the old guard at CBS did not think Dylan could play or sing and they dubbed him "Hammond's folly".

Eddie Cochran was at Liberty. Chuck Berry and the other raw rock talent were on small jazz and R&B labels — Dot, Sun, Chess, Specialty, Atlantic/Atco and Atlantic. The new sound was coming out of young companies like the Philles label that Phil Spector formed with Lester Sill in 1961 and Berry Gordy's Tamla Motown, formed in 1959.

In Great Britain, the giants, EMI and Decca, were more progressive. They were looking for an English answer to Elvis. They came up with Cliff Richard who made his mark at home, but did not break into the American charts until 1979.

EMI snapped up the Hollies, the Animals, the Dave Clark Five, Herman's Hermits, the Yardbirds, Gerry and the Pacemakers, Billy J. Kramer and the Dakotas — and an obscure little group called the Beatles, which they assigned to their comedy label, Parlophone. Decca had Billy Fury, Brian Poole and the Tremeloes, and the Rolling Stones.

THE "ENGLISH INVASION"

In the United States, Capitol made a gesture towards the new music by signing the Beach Boys, but the Beatles had to be forced on them by EMI. Once the Beatles took off, the English invasion was in full swing.

Decca was best placed to take advantage of this with its London label in the United States, while EMI continued to have trouble with Capitol. Between 1963 and 1965 EMI had 15 chart-topping acts in the United States, but Capitol took only three of them. Matters began to improve when EMI took control of Capitol in 1971.

Columbia was still not convinced that rock and roll was here to stay. As late as 1965 it had only Bob Dylan, Paul Revere and the Raiders, Simon and Garfunkel, and the Byrds. Then, in 1967, Clive Davis fought his way to the top at Columbia and at the Monterey Pop Festival that year, the "summer of love", he got rock and roll like others get religion.

Lou Adler of Ode Records took him there. Davis had signed a distribution deal with Ode that first bore fruit with Scott McKenzie's "San Francisco (Be Sure to Wear Some Flowers in Your Hair)".

The "hippie heaven" festival turned into a feeding frenzy, with the majors snapping up unsigned talent. Dylan's manager, Albert Grossman, took Steve Miller and the Quicksilver Messenger Service to Capitol and Jimi Hendrix to Warners. He took Janis Joplin to Davis for $100,000. Davis also came out of the festival with Moby Grape, Tom Rush, the Association and Laura Nyro. These signings put Columbia on the rock route that took them from five floors at 799 Seventh Avenue, with small offices in four foreign countries, to their "Black Rock" headquarters, branch offices in Nashville and Los Angeles and subsidiaries in some 50 countries.

Meanwhile, black music exploded, first through white-owned companies like Stax, then through one black-owned company — Motown.

RIGHT: In the sixties, British teenagers brought European style to rock and roll. These four hepcats are pictured in London's Speakeasy club, a retreat of many rock stars of the era.

STAX

Among fans of black music in the 1960s, Stax was a legend. Its headquarters were a disused movie theatre in Memphis with a sign outside in giant, red plastic letters: "SOULSVILLE U.S.A."

The label was started by an unlikely couple – a white brother and sister, a banker and a school teacher, Jim Stewart and Estelle Axton – at a time when the South was so strictly segregated that Jim Stewart says he never met a black person until he was full-grown.

Soul brother and sister

Estelle moved to Memphis from Middleton, Tennessee, in 1934, married, had kids and taught school. Her brother, 12 years younger, followed her to Memphis, after a stint in the Special Services, to study business at Memphis State University and prepare for a banking career. After graduating from college in 1956, he joined the First National Bank in the bonds department.

But Stewart was a musician. He had always played the fiddle. He moonlighted in several western swing bands and played at a club called the Clearpool where the unknown Elvis Presley performed during the interval.

In 1957 he started fooling around with recording in his wife's uncle's garage on Orchard Street with some equipment lent to him by a friend. His first single was "Blue Roses", sung by a local DJ called Fred Bylar. Bylar's radio connections were not enough to get it airplay.

Despite that early setback, Stewart was determined to press ahead. He turned to his sister for help and Estelle raised $2,500 by

ABOVE: **Otis Redding was working as a chauffeur when he travelled to Memphis with singer Johnny Jenkins for an audition with Stax. At the end of Jenkins's session, Redding was allowed to sing two songs. One of them was "These Arms of Mine", released by Stax in 1962. In 1967, he teamed up with the Queen of Soul for the album "King and Queen".**

RIGHT: **Ray Charles's development of the soul sound at Atlantic was enormously important for Stax. And his influence was constantly refreshed by the two-way exchange of talent between Stax in Memphis and Atlantic in New York.**

RIGHT: **Eddie Floyd's first hit at Stax was "Knock on Wood", which reached number 28 in 1966. The album of the same name was released in 1967. Floyd also wrote songs for Wilson Pickett and Carla Thomas, and toured America and Europe with the Stax Revue.**

taking out a second mortgage on her home – enough to buy an Ampex monaural recorder.

"Blue Roses" had been issued on the Satellite label – satellites were much in the news at the time – but Stewart soon discovered that there was another Satellite on the West Coast. So the company he set up with his sister changed its name to Stax – from the first two letters of their surnames, Stewart and Axton. It was to become one of the biggest labels for black music in the mid-1960s.

Jim and Estelle began recording at weekends in a warehouse in Brunswick. Their first "signing" was a rock group from Messick High School called the Royal Spades, formed by Estelle's son, Packy. Estelle set up an ice-cream stand to bring in money and began travelling out of the city to unearth new talent.

Change of direction

Stax suddenly changed direction when Jim and Estelle heard Ray Charles' "What'd I Say" and added rhythm and blues to their country and rockabilly output. They even found a distributor, Mercury, for their R&B output. But their early recordings did nothing.

Many people claim that Stax's change of fortune resulted from the move to Memphis in 1960. There Jim found the Capitol, an old movie theatre on East McLemore that had been used for country and western shows, but was now standing empty. Jim and Estelle took it for $100 a

week, ripped out the seats and installed a control room. They padded the walls, carpetted the floor and hung up acoustic curtains that Estelle ran up at home.

This curious recording studio is probably responsible for Stax's unique sound. The sloping floor and the bass-heavy U-8 movie-house speakers made everything sound better on playback. But their new city location gave Stax another advantage. They could sell records direct from the old cinema's sweet and popcorn booth, which they converted into the Satellite Records store.

The "oldest teenager in the world"

Then the self-proclaimed "oldest teenager in the world", the 43-year-old Rufus Thomas, came by. He had started in a minstrel show as a child and had recorded with Sam Phillips at Sun before being dropped for the young Elvis Presley. Thomas continued to stock boilers at a textile bleaching factory, a job he had had for 20 years, to keep his wife and four kids.

But Thomas was a powerhouse. He recorded for local labels and DJed on local radio stations. And in a few years the middle-aged Thomas would be teaching the Rolling Stones how to walk the dog.

He came to Stax to record a duet called "Cause I Love You" with his 17-year-old daughter, Carla. Booker T. played sax. "Cause I Love You" got a great deal of airplay and was a minor hit in the South, selling nearly 20,000 copies. It came to the attention of Atlantic. Jerry Wexler leased the record and took a five-year option on future duets. Stax had made its first $1,000.

Carla Thomas's first solo, "Ghee Whiz", gave Stax its first hit and the label began a healthy two-way deal with Atlantic. Wexler sent artists south to record at Stax, while local Stax talent was distributed by Atlantic in New York and Fame in Muscle Shoals.

The Royal Spades turned into the Markeys, then – with the addition of Booker T. Jones – into Booker T. and the MGs. In the segregated South, Stax was a blip of integration and the labels roster was soon bursting with fresh talent.

STAX

6513-11
Pub. East

"THE DOG"
(Rufus Thomas)
RUFUS THOMAS

DISTRIBUTED BY ATLANTIC RECORD SALES, 1841 BROADWAY N

RIGHT: **Rufus Thomas and his daughter Carla established Stax as a major label. He brought with him an R&B pedigree that stretched back to the forties. His first national hit was "Bear Cat" on the Sun label in 1953.**

OPPOSITE LEFT: **Carla Thomas was dubbed the Queen of Soul before Aretha Franklin assumed the title. Her first hit was "Gee Whiz" in 1961. Reaching number 10 in the pop charts and number five in the R&B charts, its national success put the Memphis soul label on the map.**

BELOW: **After "Bear Cat", Rufus Thomas's success with animals continued. In 1963, "The Dog" reached 22 in the R&B charts and "Walking the Dog" reached 10 in the pop charts and five in the R&B charts. And in 1973, he followed up with "Do the Funky Chicken", which reached 31 in the pop charts and five in the R&B charts.**

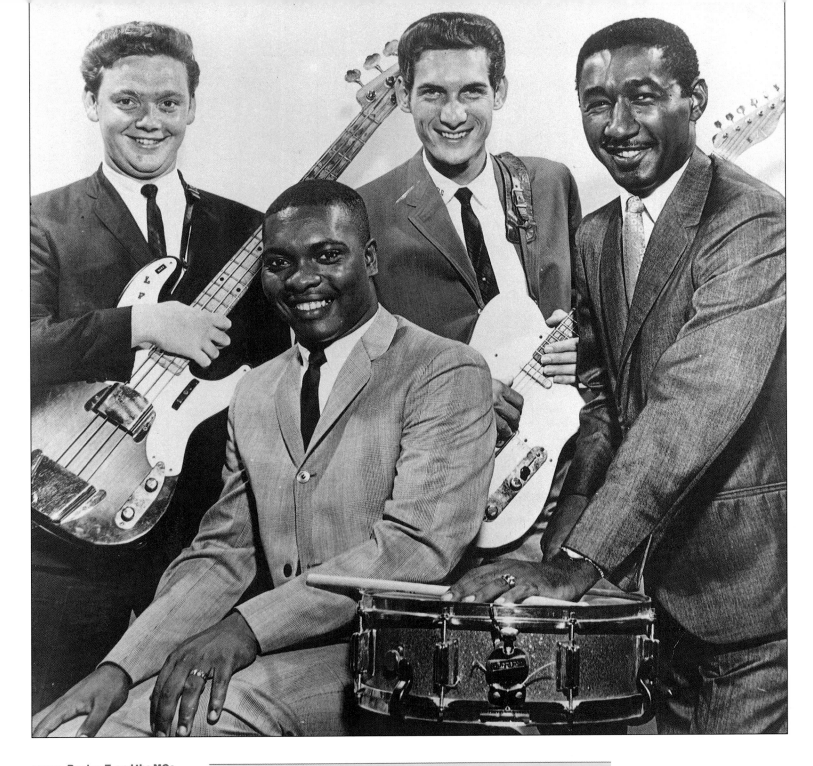

ABOVE: **Booker T. and the MGs were Stax's house band and were largely responsible for the punchy Stax sound. Along with their own recordings, such as "Green Onions", they provided the backing for Stax and Atlantic artists Otis Redding, Sam and Dave, Rufus Thomas and Wilson Pickett.**

FROM STUDIO TO STREET AND BACK

Jim Stewart and the other technicians and musicians from Stax hung about in the record store or served behind the counter in their free time. Not only did this bring in much needed cash, it gave them instant feedback from record-buyers. Fledgling musicians would drop in on the off-chance. Local kids like David Porter and Booker T. Jones were often found there. Porter, who bagged up groceries in Jones Big Star Store across the street, later became a songwriter for Sam and Dave and for Isaac Hayes. Jones went to the local church and later formed Booker T. and the MGs.

STAX

Otis Redding

One day in 1963 a Little Richard impersonator whom everyone dismissed as a lousy singer stopped by for a recording session. No one had much confidence. But he sang a ballad and Jim Stewart spotted a curious quaver in voice. His name was Otis Redding. Stax entered a whole new phase and Redding pumped out hit after hit.

By 1967 Stax was touring Europe with Otis Redding, Arthur Conley, Sam and Dave, Booker T. and the MGs, Eddie Floyd and Carla Thomas. In Great Britain, the Beatles sent limos to pick up the artists from the airport. They took time off from recording *Sergeant Pepper's Lonely Hearts Club Band* to see Carla Thomas. And when they met her, they bowed from the waist in unison.

Then tragedy struck. On 10 December, 1967, Otis Redding was killed in a plane crash in Wisconsin. A small record company like Stax could not easily bounce back from the death of its major star. They were just recovering when, on 4 April, 1968, Martin Luther King was assassinated. The atmosphere suddenly changed. A white business in a black neighbourhood, Stax shut down for a time.

Soon Stax was reeling from another blow. Atlantic was sold to Warner Brothers and Jim Stewart soon discovered that Warners now owned the masters of everything they had recorded so far. Stax was forced into a deal with Paramount Pictures Music Division.

BELOW: **Samuel Moore and David Prater – Sam and Dave – both sang in church and were solo singers on the chitlin' circuit before teaming up in the early sixties. They first signed to Roulette, but moved to Stax in 1965. There they had a string of 13 soul hits, largely written by Stax house writers Isaac Hayes and David Porter.**

BELOW: **Otis Redding became, more than any other artist, the sound of Stax. He had 15 R&B hits during his short career, much of his material co-written with Stax session guitarist Steve Cropper or fellow soul singer Jerry Butler. He also produced Arthur Conley at Stax and eventually set up his own label, Jotis.**

BELOW: Isaac Hayes was a Stax session musician and house songwriter until the label's Enterprise subsidiary gave him a break. His lavish arrangements subtly transformed soul into disco. In 1974, he moved on to the ABC label.

RIGHT: The Staples—Roebuck "Pop" Staples and his three daughters, Cleo, Mavis and Yvonne—began as a gospel group, recording on the Vee Jay label. They tried to move into the secular market on Epic, but the new commercial approach did not work until they signed to Stax in 1968.

STAX

The hits nevertheless kept coming. Johnnie Taylor's "Who's Making Love" sold more than two million copies, the biggest Stax hit ever. Luther Ingram recorded "If Loving You is Wrong". But black artists were growing wary of white executives and Ingram's manager, Johnny Baylor, and his bodyguard, the intimidating "Boom, Boom", moved in on the business.

Stax session man, Isaac Hayes, was given his chance and cut the triple-platinum album, *Hot Buttered Soul*. But this turned out to be a disaster. Hayes was not under contract to make albums and it came out instead on the Enterprise label. Then Booker T. left for California.

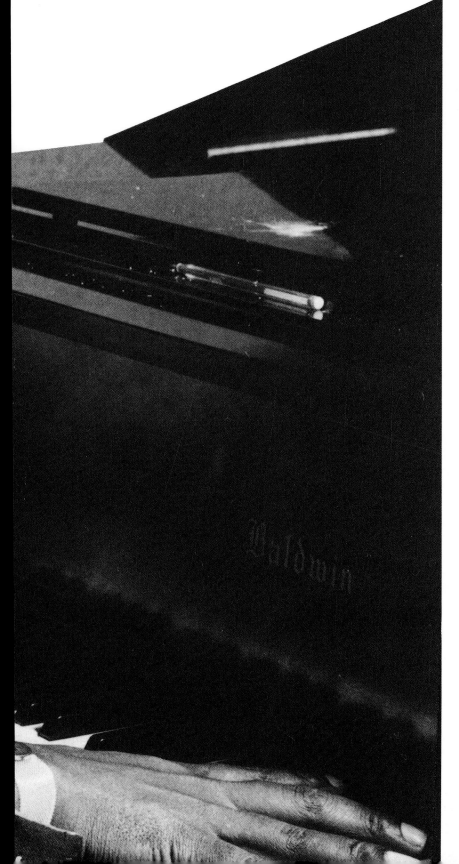

Fighting to survive

In July, 1970, with money borrowed from Deutsche Grammophon, Jim Stewart and Al Bell repurchased the company from Paramount. Within a year, they had repaid DGG, but the buyouts and payouts proved wearisome. In 1972 Al Bell began negotiations with Columbia.

Anti-trust laws prevented Columbia from taking over Stax; instead, they began a distribution deal and their input of money allowed Bell to push out Stewart. Much of the talent had dispersed, though Stax continued to have hits with Rufus Thomas, Isaac Hayes, the Staples, the Soul Children and Johnnie Taylor and it brought on the newcomers, Mel and Tim, Rance Allen, the Emotions and Fredrick Knight and Jean Knight. Even the comedian, Richard Pryor, recorded his debut album, *That Nigger's Crazy*, on the Stax subsidiary, Partee.

Stax latched on to the black-consciousness movement by organizing Wattstax in 1972, a concert at the Los Angeles Coliseum, to commemorate the Watts uprising seven years earlier. Stax, with its CBS affiliation, sold a double album and a movie off the event.

Although much of the money was donated to Jackson's Operation PUSH, the Sickle Cell Anemia Foundation and the Martin Luther King Hospital in Watts, local people in Memphis asked what Stax was doing for them. Then Johnny Baylor was stopped at Memphis airport with a suitcase full of cash. The Internal Revenue Service moved in. Artists like Isaac Hayes began to sue the company. Stax tried to generate cash-flow by creating new labels that, they claimed, were outside the CBS distribution deal. This brought a suit from CBS.

In Stax's books, Internal Revenue agents uncovered the promotional backhanders that were commonplace in the record business. And despite, or because of, the massively expensive signings of the British child star, Lena Zavaroni, and others, Stax could no longer pay the bills and slipped into bankruptcy on 12 January, 1976.

MOTOWN

For many, Tamla Motown was the sound of the sixties. It was certainly the most successful black-owned record company ever.

The man behind it was Berry Gordy. He was the son of a farmer from Georgia who had moved north in 1922 to escape the lynchings which were at an all-time high in that era.

Berry Gordy III was born in Detroit in 1929. The young Gordy was a boxer and worked out with Golden Gloves champion, Jackie Wilson. After a stint in the US Army, he went to work as a $90-a-week chrome-trimmer on the production line at Ford and began to develop an interest in music – jazz at first, then R&B.

BELOW: **Motown's Berry Gordy became a role model for a generation of black entrepreneurs. And after the success of Motown, black artists were no longer content to be exploited by white businessmen when they could be ripped off by one of their own.**

ABOVE: **Motown became a cross between a finishing school and a Detroit-style production line. The result was a new sound of black America which appealed directly to a white audience.**

OPPOSITE: **Jackie Wilson's 1957 number one "Reet Petite" was written by Berry Gordy and gave Motown's founder his first taste of success. It was a hit again in 1987, 12 years after Wilson had fallen into a terminal coma.**

RIGHT: Never in the history of pop music was so much talent concentrated in one place at one time. But Motown was more than a record company. In the sixties, it became a symbol of the new aspirations of black people.

BELOW RIGHT: The brown and yellow label became the cornerstone of every sixties teenager's record collection. The Marvelettes came straight to Motown from high school, introduced to Berry Gordy by their teacher.

Wilson had replaced Clyde McPhatter as lead singer of the Domi-noes. When he went solo in 1957, Gordy started writing for him. He wrote "Reet Petite", which reached number 67 in the United States and number six in Great Britain, "I'll be Satisfied" and "Lonely Tear-drops", his first million-seller. He also wrote "You Got What It Takes" for Marv Johnson.

With $700 borrowed from his sister, Gordy formed a production company and recorded Johnson and Smokey Robinson, whose back-ing group, the Matadors, Gordy renamed the Miracles. They recorded Gordy's "Got a Job", a gimmicky sequel to the Silhouettes's hit, "Get a Job". It reached number one in the R&B charts, but Gordy earned just $3.19 in royalties. He wrote and recorded "Money" by Barrett Strong for his sister's label, Anna, which was distributed by Chess. But Robinson convinced Gordy that he could do better if he had a record label of his own instead of recording for others.

So Gordy started Tamla – it was to have been called Tammy, until Gordy discovered there was already a record label of that name. That was followed by Motown – named for Detroit, the centre of the American motor industry – Soul and Gordy. He also established pub-lishing and management companies that handled every aspect of an artist's career, largely to the benefit of Motown. Diana Ross described the Artist's Development Department as a "sort of finishing school".

MOTOWN

OPPOSITE: **Smokey Robinson and the Miracles. Robinson provided much of the creative muscle behind Tamla Motown and became the label's musical director. He was made vice-president.**

Smokey Robinson handled artist development and Mary Wells gave the label its first hits. Smokey Robinson and the Miracles followed. "Way Over There" was realized in mid-1959 and "Shop Around" gave Tamla its first gold record. The Marvelettes also went gold with "Please Mister Postman", the company's first number one.

The Tamla team had found that the key to commercial success was softening the sexual element in raw rhythm and blues to make it more acceptable to the white teenage market. Robinson became in-house music director and Henry Fuqua and Marvin Gaye joined the

ABOVE: **The line-up for Motown's 1965 tour of Britain (from left to right): the Temptations, Stevie Wonder, the Supremes, and Martha Reeves and the Vandellas.**

LEFT: **It was Smokey Robinson who persuaded Berry Gordy to start Motown. After three hits with other labels, Smokey Robinson and the Miracles moved on to Gordy's new label. They gave Motown 44 hits.**

LEFT: **The Detroit-based Four Tops first signed to Chess in 1956, but switched labels when their old friend Berry Gordy established Motown. From 1965 to 1972, they were one of Motown's most consistent hitmakers. Then they left to go to ABC/Dunhill where they produced another three new top-10 hits.**

MOTOWN

MOTOWN

company when they married Gordy's sisters. This close family control made the company intensely secretive. Many Motown million-sellers were not registered as gold by the Record Industry Association of America because Motown would not let outsiders examine their books. By 1964 Motown was the largest independent label in the United States with 42 best-selling records and sales of over 12 million. They signed other acts who had already made a name for themselves on other labels – like Gladys Knight and the Pips and the Isley Brothers. And the sales figures went on increasing.

But not everyone was happy with Gordy's autocratic style. Mary Wells, Kim Weston, Martha Reeves, Holland-Dozier-Holland, Jimmy Ruffin and the Four Tops quit. But few had much success after leaving. Only the Detroit Spinners went on to greater success.

The lead singer of the Supremes, Florence Ballard, quit and later died on welfare. Gordy replaced her with Diana Ross, whom he groomed to be the black Barbara Streisand.

Being family, Marvin Gaye was in a position to control his own destiny. He began producing LPs rather than pop singles. And Stevie Wonder, who had first signed to the label as a minor, was already an established star when he turned 21. He was therefore able to renegotiate a contract that would keep him with Motown and generate a roster of hits.

Though Gordy gave up control in the studio, he continued to control the company itself. He launched a white rock label, Rare Earth, with the band of the same name. It is significant that, for years, the distribution vice-president, Barney Ales, was Motown's only white employee. Many people thought he owned the company.

A HIT FACTORY

Gordy ran the company like a production line. He owned the names of the Motown groups and insisted on life-long performance contracts. Local Detroit talent was encouraged and artists were paid a salary until they had a hit. The company's roster soon included the Supremes, the Jackson Five, the Four Tops, the Temptations, Little Stevie Wonder, Martha and the Vandellas, Junior Walker and the Marvelettes. Acts were groomed and taught deportment, their stages acts choreographed and their tours tightly chaperoned. Song-writing teams included Ashford and Simpson, Holland-Dozier-Holland and Robinson himself. Staff producers included Gordy, Fuqua, Robinson and Johnny Bristol. Together they produced a sound that dominated the R&B charts and appealed to a white audience. Their output became known as the sound of young America. Quite simply, Motown became a hit factory.

ABOVE: Like so many of the girl groups of the sixties, Martha Reeves and the Vandellas were a product of Motown's Artists' Development Department, which taught unworldly young musicians how to handle public attention as well as stagecraft. Reeves moved to MCA as a solo act in 1972.

LEFT: Legend has it that Diana Ross discovered the Jackson Five and brought them to Berry Gordy. Michael, seated, was eight in 1970 when the Jacksons were signed to Motown. They left to join Epic in 1976, where Michael Jackson developed his solo career under the direction of Quincy Jones.

OPPOSITE: Marvin Gaye's big break in the music business was marrying Berry Gordy's sister, Anna. Although he had already proved his remarkable voice in a talent contest and with Henry Fuqua's Marquees who recorded on Chess, at Motown he started as a session drummer. But in 1962, he recorded "Stubborn Kind of Fellow", backed by Martha Reeves and the Vandellas, and never looked back. He produced 26 hit singles.

PLASTIC MAN
(N. Whitfield)

© 1973 Motown
Record Corporation

G 7129F
(62151)
Time 4:45

GORDY

Trademark Motown
Record Corporation

THE TEMPTATIONS

In Album: "MASTERPIECE"
G 965L

Stone Diamond
Music Corp. (BMI)
© 1973 Stone
Diamond Music
Corp.
Produced by
Norman Whitfield
Arranged by
Paul Riser

A Product Of Motown Record Corporation

MOTOWN

Unpaid royalties

In 1971 Holland-Dozier-Holland sued Motown for what they claimed were more than $22 million in back royalties. Other artists also questioned the sales figures and were put on suspension. Martha Reeves later said that she had never earned more than $200 a week during her time at Motown and her new label, MCA, had to pay more than $200,000 to cover what Gordy described as "advance debits". Paul Wilson, the original lead singer of the Temptations, was put on "permanent suspension" after his confrontation with Gordy. He later committed suicide.

When the white singer, Teena Maria, signed to Motown, she had no attorney to advise her. And when she asked to take the contract home so that her parents could examine it, she was asked: "Don't you trust us?" Motown made an estimated $2 million from two of her albums, while Teena got just $100 a week for her six and a half years with the company.

In 1971 Gordy moved the whole company to Los Angeles. In the move Motown somehow lost its soul. The music became smoother, more commercial and less funky. Gladys Knight, the Isley Brothers and the Jackson Five all left the label. But still Motown's success continued. In 1973 the company grossed $40 million and employed 135 people. And when Stevie Wonder's contract was up for grabs in 1975, Gordy managed to secure it with a bid of $13 million.

Through all the changes Motown had become just another – though a major – record label. A distribution deal was signed with MCA; then, in 1988, MCA and outside investors bought out Motown for just $61 million.

After the sale Diana Ross returned to the label, taking payment in stock instead of cash. She still feels that the company has much to offer the up-and-coming young stars of the future.

OPPOSITE: **The careers of the Temptations and the Supremes were constantly refreshed with new styles and new material. Gordy wielded such a powerful creative influence because his companies managed the acts as well as recorded them.**

ABOVE: **Gladys Knight and the Pips had successes on Brunswick and Maxx before signing to Motown in 1966. "I Heard It Through the Grapevine" shot to number two in the US and started them on the road to international success. Their career continued to flourish after they moved to Buddah, and was further revitalized when they signed to Columbia in 1980.**

BELOW: **The Isley Brothers began singing gospel in their home town of Cincinnati. In 1959, they signed with RCA and had a number of hits, including "Twist and Shout" which was covered by the Beatles. Their four years with Motown, from 1965 to 1969, was the most successful period in their career, establishing their international reputation. After 1969, they recorded for their own label, T-Neck.**

MOTOWN

DECCA

LEFT: Stevie Wonder is one of the few Motown artists who stuck with the company. First signing at the age of 10, he was able, as an established star, to renegotiate terms when he came of age legally at 21.

BELOW: In 1932, Decca bought the British subsidiary of Brunswick, which first gave them access to the recordings of Bing Crosby. Crosby later signed to American Decca.

T he Decca name first made its appearance on portable record players that were popular in the trenches during the First World War. But it did not become a record label until 1929, when it was taken over by the stockbroker, Edward Lewis, who also bought the failing Duophone label. Lewis was to run Decca for the next 50 years.

BOTTOM: Decca always prided itself on technical excellence, even lending its expertise to the wartime development of radar. The cost of such patriotism meant that Decca lost its American arm.

BELOW LEFT: Decca moved into the record business in 1929 and went on to become the second biggest record company in the world. Only EMI was bigger.

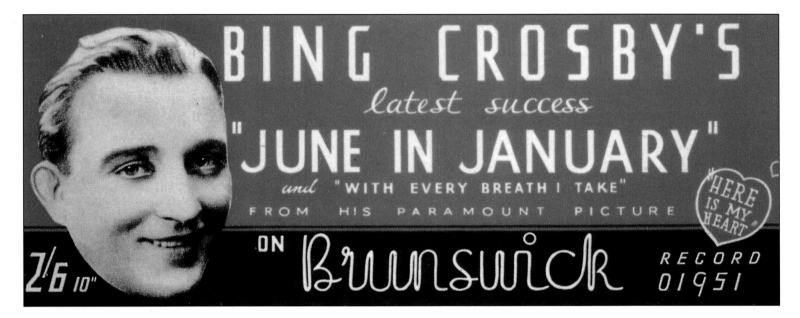

DECCA

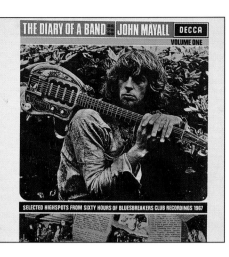

ABOVE: **Decca's finest hour was the sixties. While EMI had the popsters, Decca recorded the harline British R&B bands, including the Rolling Stones and John Mayall's Bluesbreakers — with Eric Clapton — and later, Mayall on his own.**

The Decca label first recorded British bandleaders like Jack Hylton, Billy Cotton and Ambrose. Then, in 1932, they bought the UK subsidiary of Brunswick, which gave them British rights to Al Jolson and Bing Crosby. This brought in enough revenue to enable the label to start taking over other Depression-hit American companies, this time in the United States itself.

In 1933 Decca bought Edison Bell Winner. It tried to take over Columbia for just $200,000 in 1934, but was beaten by the American company, ARC. But Decca did succeed in snapping up Rex, Imperial and Vocalion in 1937.

In the wake of the failed bid for Columbia, Lewis had set up American Decca. Jack Knapp from Brunswick headed the new operation. Under his aegis, American Decca soon had Louis Armstrong, Guy Lombardo, the Mills Brothers and Bing Crosby. And Decca USA became the second biggest record company in the United States when Kapp slashed the price of records to just 35 cents, half the previous cost.

In 1942 the Decca recording of Bing Crosby's "White Christmas" became the biggest seller of all time — until Michael Jackson came along. But the war intervened in the label's progress. Decca UK's electronic arm was instrumental in developing radar, which the company paid for by selling shares in Decca USA. This made the American company practically autonomous until the 1960s, when it was taken

LEFT: **The Decca name was closely associated with popular music for more than 60 years. The trademark was first seen on a portable gramophone made by Barnett Samuel & Sons, popular in the trenches during the First World War.**

BELOW: **Decca's recording of "White Christmas" caught the mood in the winter of 1942 when British and American armies were fighting the Germans in North Africa.**

RIGHT: **During Decca's golden era of the sixties, the London label was Decca's US agent. London also aped Decca's slogan, promising "full frequency" stereo sound.**

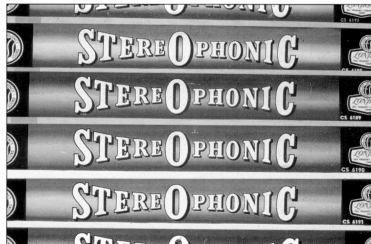

ABOVE: **In 1934, American Decca was established by Jack Knapp, who brought with him two of Brunswick's major stars: Bing Crosby and Louis Armstrong. This assured the success of the fledgeling label.**

DECCA

over by the Music Company of America (until that time a booking agency) and became the hub of the MCA label.

Decca UK maintained links with the American operation until 1974, but as early as 1947 Lewis established a new outlet in the United States, London Records. London exported Gracie Fields and Vera Lynn, who became the first British artist to have a number one hit in the United States with "Auf Wiedersehen".

British rock and roll

Its American outlet put Decca in the perfect position when Great Britain began to respond to the rock-and-roll revolution. The label's first export of that era was the British million-seller, Lonnie Donegan, who had a hit in the United States, ironically with the Hubbie "Leadbelly" Ledbetter song, "Rock Island Line".

Decca had Great Britain's first rock-and-roll stars – Tommy Steele, Billy Fury and the Tornados. "Telstar", the Tornados instrumental named after the telecommunications satellite that transmitted phone calls and television pictures between the United States and Europe for the first time, became the third British record to reach number one in the United States.

Though Decca seemed to have the golden touch, it made the same mistake that practically every other label did in the early 1960s – it turned down the Beatles. Instead, it signed Brian Poole and the Tremeloes and, later the Rolling Stones.

The Decca/London tie-up worked the other way round, too. While Decca was taking British bands to the United States, London brought Bobby Darin, the Everly Brothers, Ricky Nelson, Duane Eddy, Little Richard, Ike and Tina Turner, the Ronettes, the Crystals, Del Shannon, Eddie Cochran and Roy Orbison to Great Britain. In addition, Decca

DECCA

was responsible for the worldwide success of traditional crooners Engelbert Humperdinck and Tom Jones.

By the end of the 1960s, the best was over for Decca. Sir Edward Lewis was getting old and in 1970 the Rolling Stones left Decca to form their own label. RCA, which had leased its material to Decca in Great Britain, followed the example of other American companies and set up their own British operation in 1971. The Moody Blues were the only pop act that Decca had left in the 1970s. And when Lewis died in 1980, PolyGram took over the remnants.

LEFT: **The jewel in Decca's crown was the Rolling Stones. They brought Sir Edward Lewis's old established company a new street cred — and a new penetration into America.**

EMI

EMI is Great Britain's music giant, the biggest recording company in the world for nearly 50 years. The Beatles immortalized its London recording studios in Abbey Road, opened in November, 1931. EMI itself had been formed just eight months earlier, in March, 1931, but its history really started with the beginning of recorded sound.

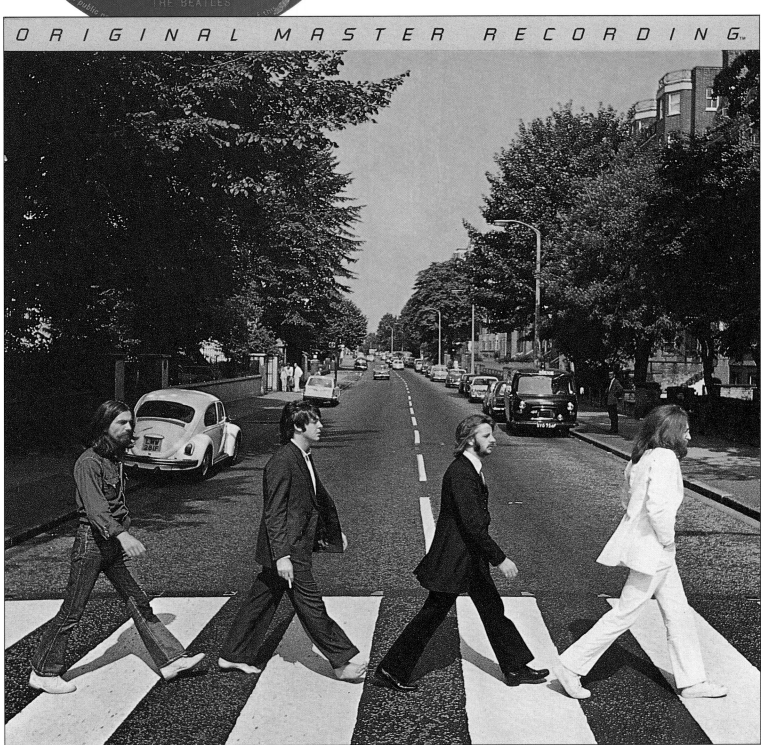

EMI/PARLOPHONE'S CRUCIAL SIGNING

It was clear to company head Joseph Lockwood that rock was the profit-centre of the future and EMI began casting around for native British rock-and-roll talent. In 1958 EMI signed Cliff Richard and the Shadows. The Beatles sent demo tapes to the company, but they were rejected. But when the group's new manager, Brian Epstein, took material to EMI again, the band was assigned to the Parlophone label. The date of that historic signing was 6 June, 1962.

Parlophone had originally been part of Holland's the Transoceanic Trading Company, set up during the First World War to look after German interests overseas. When EMI took it over they used it to issue novelty and comedy records. Peter Sellers recorded comic monologues for Parlophone. The Beatles gave the producer, George Martin, the opportunity to turn Parlophone into the seminal pop label of the Swinging London era. And the Beatles knocked Cliff Richard off the top of the charts in 1964.

ABOVE: In the late fifties, the best of the British Elvis imitators was Cliff Richard. He has been a consistent hitmaker for EMI in the UK for over 30 years, but has had only a handful of hits in the US.

In 1898 the inventor of the gramophone, Emile Berliner, founded The Gramophone Company. Two years later he registered the famous picture of Nipper the dog listening to a gramophone as the trademark of His Master's Voice – HMV – in Great Britain and the United States. The painting had originally shown Nipper listening to a phonograph – a cylinder machine, the direct rival of Berliner's disc-playing gramophone. The artist, Francis Barraud, was paid £100 for the picture – £50 for the painting itself and £50 for the copyright – provided that a gramophone was substituted for the phonograph.

The other arm of EMI was even older. It began with Columbia, the oldest record label still in existence. On 1 January, 1889, Edward Easton incorporated a company called the North American Phonograph, which leased and serviced dictating machines, based on Edison's phonograph, in the District of Columbia. North America's other 33 franchise failed, but Columbia survived by selling recordings. By 1891 it was the biggest recording company in the world, with a catalogue of 200 recordings, all on cylinder.

By 1900 it had opened a London office and was pressing both cylinders and discs. But the economic recession after the First World

TOP LEFT: The red Parlophone label was EMI's comedy subsidiary, but under the management of George Martin it managed to grab most of the talent coming out of Liverpool in the early sixties, including the Beatles. In the US, "Please Please Me" appeared on Vee Jay and Capitol.

LEFT: Even after the Beatles set up their own Apple label, their distribution deals with EMI and Capitol made a major contribution to profits.

RIGHT: The later black Parlophone label also carried the Beatles output. "She Loves You" appeared in the US on Swan and Capitol. It was the Beatles's first US hit.

EMI

War forced the company to sell its British subsidiary to its manager, Louis Sterling, in 1922. When Columbia failed in the United States in 1923, Sterling bought it to get his hands on Western Electric's new electrical recording processes, which were available only to American companies. Like its rival, HMV, the London-based Columbia International soon expanded worldwide.

In the United States, Columbia moved into broadcasting. But the company was badly hit by the Depression. The Columbia Broadcasting System, CBS, became independent, while the rest of the group merged with Sterling's HMV to form Electrical and Music Industries, EMI. Columbia remained its flagship pop label, outside the United States, and maintained a stake in RCA Victor until 1957.

In 1931 the only record companies not in the EMI empire were Brunswick in the United States, Decca in Great Britain and Deutsche Grammophon Gesellschaft, the rump of Berliner's original Gramophone company, in Germany. DGG had the right to use HMV's Nipper the Dog trademark in Germany after the company had been seized as enemy property in the First World War. Not until the Second World War did EMI win back the right to use Nipper in Germany. Meanwhile, EMI's newly established German subsidiary, Electrola, has its first million-seller with "Lille Marlene".

Speed war

During the speed war of the late 1940s, when LPs and 45s replaced the old-fashioned 78s, EMI lagged behind the field. Decca began issuing LPs and, eager to exploit the new format, many of EMI's artists defected. RCA brought EMI some of Elvis Presley's early hits, before switching its licensing to Decca, but CBS also pulled out of its licensing arrangement with EMI, switching to Philips, leaving EMI without any access to any of the rock-and-roll artists who were beginning to make an impression in the mid-fifties.

A former flour-milling engineer, Joseph Lockwood, took over the levers of control at EMI and bought Capitol Records in 1955. He was criticized for paying too much, but four years later Capitol was worth £85 million, nearly 30 times what he paid for it.

Billy J. Kramer and the Dakotas, the Hollies and Cilla Black were also signed by Parlophone. Along with Cliff Richard, EMI had Manfred Mann on HMV, the Move and Joe Cocker on Regal-Zonophone and the Animals, the Yardbirds, the Dave Clarke Five, Frank Ifield, Peter and Gordon, Georgie Fame and the Seekers on Columbia – not to mention the Beach Boys on Capitol.

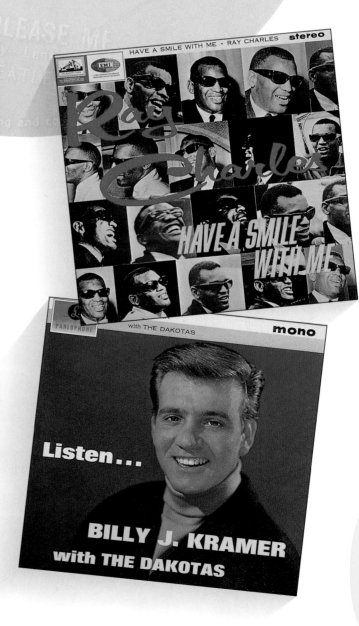

ABOVE: **Sheffield-born gasfitter Joe Cocker first appeared as a supporting act for the Rolling Stones. But his debut on Decca was a flop and it was only later, on EMI's Regal-Zonophone label, that Cocker established his soulful reputation.**

EMI

Number one in Great Britain

EMI artists held the number one spot in the British charts for 76 weeks in 1963 and 1964. But EMI's American subsidiary, Capitol, refused to handle most of them. Even the Beatles had to be forced on Capitol.

The huge profits built up in the 1960s were quickly frittered away in diversification. For EMI, the 1970s were a nightmare. Capitol ran up huge losses and WEA, CBS and RCA all began to compete on home ground, setting up British subsidiaries. EMI could not fight back, because the Labour government prevented British firms from making overseas investments.

In 1979 the whole of the ailing EMI was taken over by Thorn Electrical Industries. The new owners left EMI largely alone and soon its luck began to change. It took over Imperial, Liberty, United Artists Records and the roster of the jazz label, Blue Note, which EMI re-established in 1984.

A new roster of British talent, including David Bowie, Queen, Pink Floyd, Duran Duran, the Pet Shop Boys, Sheena Easton, Paul

ABOVE: **EMI's US subsidiary Capitol handed their parent company the Beach Boys, pictured here (with friends) in England in 1966. After Sinatra left to form his own label, the Beach Boys were Capitol's sole support until EMI forced them to take on the Beatles.**

OPPOSITE TOP: **Like its rival Decca, EMI also began to expand its predominantly UK output with US acts in the late fifties and early sixties. Ray Charles was one of them.**

OPPOSITE BOTTOM: **EMI had its ear to the ground in the UK and managed to scoop up many of the Liverpool acts, including Billy J. Kramer and the Dakotas.**

EMI

McCartney and the Rolling Stones gave EMI renewed international muscle. It established EMI America and the Manhattan label in the United States.

EMI tried to buy the RCA music division, but lost out to Germany's Bertelsmann. Then it tried to take over CBS, which would have reunited the Columbia label, only to be outbid by Sony. But EMI is still thought to be on the acquisition trail. The company seems bent on re-establishing its global hegemony.

ABOVE: **Another EMI act, the Dave Clark Five, were the second band of the "English invasion", following the Beatles on to the prestigious Ed Sullivan Show. But their career petered out in 1965.**

RIGHT: **In the early 1989s, teenage heart-throbs Duran Duran helped to boost EMI profits, and protected them from interference by their new masters, Thorn Electrical Industries.**

CAPITOL

Glenn Wallichs ran a record store on Sunset and Vine in Hollywood with his brother, Clyde. They figured that making records would be more exciting than selling them. In the autumn of 1941 Wallichs mentioned the idea to one of his best customers, the song-writer, Johnny Mercer. But they needed money to back the business.

In January, 1942, Mercer brought in Buddy DeSylva, a former song-writer who had become an executive producer at Paramount. Together, on 8 April, 1942, in Los Angeles, they formed Liberty Records, only to find that the name had already been registered by another company. So Liberty became Capitol.

West Coast pioneers

Capitol Records was the first major record label on the west coast. DeSylva, president of the new company, took little active part in the business. The vice-president was Mercer, who handled the artistic side, while Wallichs, in his capacity as secretary-treasurer, dealt with the business side.

The fledgling label immediately ran into problems when the Second World War brought a shortage of shellac. To get the raw material for pressing, old records were bought from dealers at 6 cents a pound. The story is also told that Mercer signed one band-leader, despite his lack of talent, because his father owned a shellac warehouse.

On 1 July, 1942, Capitol released its first six recordings. Two of them were hits. Soon the label was producing 20,000 records a week. "Cow Cow Boogie" by Ella Mae Morse and Freddie Slack was its first Billboard top-ten hit and its first million-seller. But following this early success, Capitol ran straight into the American Federation of Musicians' ban on recording, called on 1 August, 1942. The union's ban lasted for more than a year.

RIGHT: **Miles Davis's "Birth of Cool" in the late forties helped establish Capitol's advanced West Coast sound. But that, and some classic Sinatra recordings, failed to save the label from EMI's takeover.**

TOP RIGHT: **Gene Vincent was one of Capitol's hottest properties from the rock-and-roll explosion. But a car accident in Britain in 1960, which killed his friend Eddie Cochran and injured his already damaged leg, drove him to drink and effectively ended his career.**

CAPITOL

OPPOSITE: **Thirteen hit albums from Frank Sinatra between 1954 and 1962 bolstered Capitol's fortunes. But he left to form his own Reprise label in 1962.**

ABOVE: **Gene Vincent maintained his homely look during his greatest days with Capitol. It was, in fact, UK pop impresario Jack Good who put Vincent into black leathers at what proved to be the end of his career.**

Once the strike was over, Capitol turned itself from being a small independent, like Mercury and Imperial, into being one of the four majors. Innovative techniques, like mastering on tape and giving records to disc jockeys, was introduced. The label went public in 1946 and used the money raised to buy its own manufacturing and distribution system. During the 1949 speed war, the company covered the ground by issuing its records on all three speeds.

Though DeSylva and Mercer had left, Capitol's new president, Glenn Wallichs, had a roster that included Peggy Lee, Nat "King" Cole and Stan Kenton. Capitol moved into black pop with Nellie Lutcher and Julia Lee and recorded Miles Davis's *Birth of Cool*. Duke Ellington, Benny Goodman, Guy Lombardo and Art Tatum all recorded for Capitol.

In the 1950s Capitol had Les Paul and Mary Ford, Nelson Riddle, Billy May and Dean Martin on its lists and in April, 1953, it signed Frank Sinatra – for nothing – after Columbia had dropped him. Sinatra, whose popularity was waning, was so grateful that, even though he received no advance, he agreed to pay for his studio time.

In September, 1954, the company began to build new headquarters on Vine. The circular Capitol Tower – built as high as city regulations would allow – is now a Los Angeles landmark. From the top, "Hollywood" is flashed out in morse code 24 hours a day.

EMI takeover

While Capitol Tower was being built, Wallichs entered into negotiations with Sir Alexander Aikman of EMI. On 17 January, 1955, EMI bought 96.41 per cent of Capitol for $8.5 million. EMI's new chairman, Joseph

CAPITOL

LEFT: **Grand Funk – originally Grand Funk Railroad – gave Capitol an American heavy-metal answer to the seventies invasion of Britain's Led Zeppelin and Black Sabbath.**

Lockwood – later Sir Joseph – joined the Capitol board and Glenn Wallichs joined the EMI board. In practice, as London and Los Angeles were over 5,000 miles apart, this made little difference to the management structure.

Capitol moved into rock and roll with Gene Vincent, whose classic "Be-Bop-A-Lula" sold a million. But the company was becoming old and staid. Glenn Wallichs brought in Alan Livingston, who signed the Beach Boys. The company rejected the Beatles, who had to go to Vee Jay for their first American releases. Then, in 1964, the group's British record company, EMI, forced Capitol to take them. This carried Capitol through the rest of the 1960s.

Their huge earnings from the Beatles left Capitol complacent. The only new artists brought on were Glen Campbell, Grand Funk Railroad, The Band, Bobby Gentry and Joe South. Investments in a rack-jobbing firm and a mail-order record club proved disastrous. Capitol lost $8 million in 1971.

Wallichs was dying of cancer and Livingston left. Stan Gortikov took over management of the company and brought in Sal Ionnucci as the label's president. Unable to turn the label around, Gortikov fired Ionnucci; EMI then fired Gortikov. The company plainly neded a firm hand. EMI put Bhaskar Menon in charge of the company. He had been a personal assistant to Sir Joseph Lockwood in the 1950s, run the company's subsidiary, Gramophone Company of India, in the early 1960s, and had returned to London as managing director of EMI International. Now he was to be the man who turned Capitol round.

Profits came from the individual Beatles, the Steve Miller Band, Linda Ronstadt, Dr Hook, A Taste of Honey, Natalie Cole (Nat "King" Cole's daughter) – and the Knack, whose single "My Sharona" sold six million copies and was the biggest selling record in the United States in 1979.

A new label

In 1978 Bhaskar Menon became head of EMI Music International, headquartered in London. He started the new label, EMI America, which finally launched the veteran rocker, Cliff Richard, as a star in the United States and which also had number-one successes with Kim Carnes, Sheena Easton and Robert John.

CAPITOL

That year EMI also bought the record division of United Artists. Blue Note, Imperial and, ironically, Liberty were merged with Capitol. This brought the hugely prestigious Blue Note jazz catalogue and Kenny Rodgers to the company.

The Liberty/United Artists takeover also began Capitol's move eastwards. In 1984 Bruce Lundvall was brought in to launch the Manhattan label in New York. This was later merged with EMI America.

The 1980s brought hits from Neil Diamond (the soundtrack from *The Jazz Singer*), Tina Turner, Bob Seger, America, the Motels, the Tubes and Great White. In addition, the label had hits in the United States with British acts like Queen, Duran Duran, Paul McCartney and Pink Floyd.

In the 1990s the company stayed abreast of the times with MC Hammer. *Please Hammer Don't Hurt 'Em* topped the charts for months in the second half of 1990 and sold 15 million copies around the world.

Capitol's country roster – begun by the DJ, Cliffie Stone, with Sonny James, Tennessee Ernie Ford, Hank Thompson, Ferlin Husky and Jimmy Wakely in the 1940s – gave the label the most successful country cross-over artist ever in 1991, when Garth Brooks's third album, *Ropin' The Wind*, went to number one on the *Billboard* album charts and sold over five million copies in the United States alone.

But after 50 years in the business, Capitol has still not managed to live down a curious reputation for a record company – honesty. In a business in which "lax" accounting practices are standard – when they are not actually ripping off the artists – Ella Mae Morse claims that, after a re-issue of her early hits, she owes Capitol money.

LEFT: **Half-Mexican, half-German country-and-western singer Linda Ronstadt helped to rebuild Capitol's profits after the Beatles broke up – but only became a big star after she defected to Asylum with producer Peter Asher.**

BELOW: **The bizarre San Francisco-based band The Tubes came to Capitol after they had established their career with A&M in the late seventies. But their period in the New Wave limelight proved to be short-lived.**

APPLE

Following the death of their manager, Brian Epstein, the Beatles formed a record label as part of their Apple Corps Ltd. They invested $2 million into what was essentially a utopian venture to become an umbrella for new talent. To this extent, they succeeded in discovering some exciting and durable acts. Neil Aspinall, who had attended the Liverpool Institute with Lennon and McCartney and later became their trusted friend, confidante and world-travelling tour manager, was appointed managing director of the Apple Label. (He is still at the helm today.)

Apple issued its first release on 30 August, 1968. It was the single "Hey Jude", with "Revolution" on the B side. As the Beatles were still signed to Parlophone, EMI distributed the single in Great Britain and most of the world; Capitol handled the distribution in North America. Within a month, Apple had sold three million records worldwide.

Offices were opened in Europe and the United States. By 1969, the company had signed Mary Hopkin, Badfinger, Billy Preston, James Taylor, Doris Troy, Jackie Lomax, the Plastic Ono Band, the Modern Jazz Quartet and Radha Krishna Temple. With this impressive line-up the record company flourished. Unfortunately, the rest of Apple Corps, the planned publishing and electronics divisions, never got off the ground; and the fashion division, with its Apple Boutique at 94 Baker Street, closed down after eight months.

OPPOSITE: The Apple headquarters at 3 Savile Row was a Mecca for fans across the world long after the company had shut its doors. Though Apple still exists as a business enterprise, there are no more handouts.

BELOW: "Let It Be" was the album that precipitated the break-up of the Beatles and the demise of Apple. When Phil Spector was called in to sort out the remixing, Paul McCartney disociated himself from the project.

Apple

ABOVE: The Apple was intended to symbolise the innocent intentions of the enterprise — an enterprise in which the Beatles' money was supposed to support a plethora of new creative endeavours. But the apple was soon found to be rotten to the core.

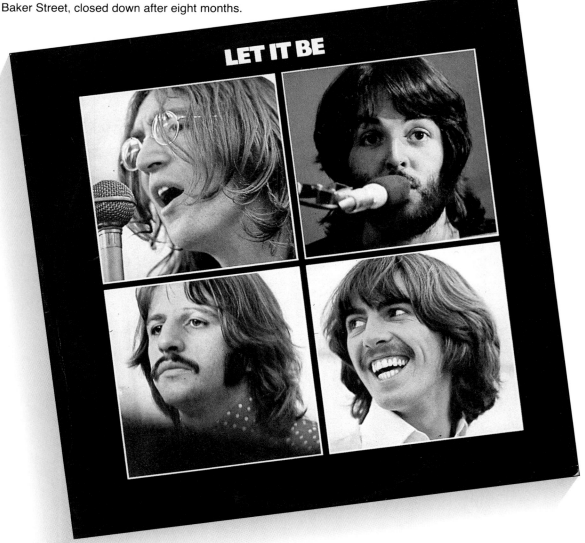

LET IT BE

APPLE

Apple's press office in 1969. Mary Hopkin sits in Derek Taylor's chair, while a broadcaster from Los Angeles waits for an interview with the Fab Four – this is his ninth day. Richard di Lello takes pictures, and why not?

Enter the businessmen

By the middle of 1969 Apple was in trouble. Record sales and the Beatles's films were bringing money in – but it was going out even quicker. No one, it seemed, was taking responsibility for an overall vision or strategy. Overstaffing, allegedly extravagant salaries and an endless supply of booze to visitors all played their part. (It was memorably summed up by former employee Robert Di Lello as "the longest cocktail party".) Being in the media spotlight brought its own problems. Beleaguered staff were forced to cope with an invasion of artists, wayfarers and good causes wanting money and the Beatle seal of approval. Both John Lennon and Paul McCartney tried separately to sort out the problem, but the growing personal and musical differences between them only exacerbated the situation. To bring Apple around, they needed the very thing the company had eschewed from the beginning: hard-nosed businessmen.

McCartney brought in the New York attorneys, Lee and John Eastman, the father and brother of his girlfriend, later wife, Linda. But Lennon did not trust them and had, in any case, already engaged the Rolling Stones fast-talking, streetwise manager, Allen Klein. Klein impressed the other two Beatles, George Harrison and Ringo Starr, and the Eastmans were part of the overall decision-making process in so far as they managed Paul's concerns.

Klein took an axe to the payroll and balanced the books; but the hippy philosophy withered on the vine. Apple stopped losing money but in the process lost its idealistic vitality and sense of purpose.

APPLE

OPPOSITE: **Apple was run by individual members of the Beatles, in strict rotation. Here George Harrison takes charge of the Apple empire in 1969, its last year.**

ABOVE: **The Beatles together in happier times, singing "Revolution". A double A-side with "Hey Jude", it was the first Beatles release on Apple. In one month, it sold over three million copies.**

By the end of the decade, the company had severely reduced its business operations.

During the seventies, a series of legal disputes over finances and song copyrights continued to mar the fortunes of the scaled-down business – even today, in 1992, Apple and EMI face each other in court over the latter's disputed right to distribute the Beatles's Red and Blue compilation albums (from 1962–7 and 1967–71 respectively).

Nevertheless, despite these wrangles, the three surviving Beatles members, and the John Lennon estate as represented by Yoko Ono, are still directors of the company. Today, Apple's chief functions are to manage the complex business matters that continually arise from the Beatles's affairs and to protect their image, copyright and merchandising interests around the world. New technology has also meant that Apple's enviable back catalogue is being released on compact disc and the other emerging media.

RIGHT: **John Lennon and Yoko Ono turn up at the Apple offices for a meeting in 1969. It would soon become clear that neither the Beatles nor Apple could hold together.**

A&M

&M was formed by an obscure session musician, Herb Alpert, and an ambitious Bronx record-promotor, Jerry Moss.

Alpert had a hit when he and his partner, Lou Adler, covered the Hollywood Argyles's 1960 West Coast regional hit, "Alley Oop". They recorded the song one day and pressed it the next. The following day it was in the stores and on American Bandstand.

The success was shortlinved. Moss joined alpert for a follow-up; it went nowhere and the label that recorded it, Madison, folded.

Moss took Alpert to the Keen label, who signed Alpert and Adler on as song-writers at $35 a week. They wrote "Wonderful World" for Sam Cooke, but, when Allen Klein took Cooke to RCA, Keen failed too. Alpert found it disheartening working for labels that constantly folded. So, with Jerry Moss, he formed his own. Its offices were Alpert's converted garage.

The company has always been artist-orientated and few people who have worked for A&M have a bad word to say about it. Its only major mistake was the signing of the Sex Pistols in 1977. EMI had just dropped the punk group after a notorious TV appearance in which they peppered the afternoon airwaves with expletives. The controversial signing was staged outside Buckingham Palace. There was a party at A&M's London office where the band disgraced itself. Staff and the labels other artists protested. Just seven days after the blaze of publicity that surrounded their signing, A&M dropped the Sex Pistols, paying them $75,000 to go away.

Alpert's own talent continued to make its contribution to A&M's success. His version of "This Guy's In Love With You" re-entered the British charts three times. Despite A&M's reputation as a middle-of-the-road label, it kept up with the latest studio technology and had two hit dance albums with *Wild Romance* and *Keep Your Eyes on Me*.

A&M was taken over by PolyGram in 1988.

TIJUANA BRASS

Herb Alpert had been a trumpeter in the US Army. He found that by overdubbing "Twinkle Star" he could produce a quasi-Mexican sound. In a recording session that cost just $200, he added bullfight crowd noises. In 1962 the renamed "Lonely Bull" went gold.

Herb Alpert's Tijuana Brass's Ameriachi sound yielded 13 hit singles in 1962—67, and 15 hit albums — five of them in the top 20 at one time in 1966. This gave A&M the money to develop new talent and its roster soon include Procol Harum, Cat Stevens, Rick Wakeman, Carole King, Phil Ochs and the Carpenters.

TOP: UK songwriter, later convert to Islam, Cat Stevens was one of the talents that A&M nurtured in the early seventies.

LEFT: Producer-performer Herb Alpert became even more adept at running his own company. A&M — Alpert and Moss — has been one of the most successful independent labels in the US.

RIGHT: **A&M records have made a success out of diversity. A creative management allows the company's artists to follow their own instincts. They even found they could veto the controversial signing of the Sex Pistols.**

ABOVE: **Procol Harum broke through in the US in the summer of love, 1967, with "A Whiter Shade of Pale" on Decca's Dream label. When A&M picked up on their next record "Homburg", they were already past their sell-by date.**

# THE SEVENTIES

The record labels moved into the seventies on a huge wave of profit. Rock was sweeping all before it. The sales of American record labels totalled $1.2 billion, twice the gross in 1960. Albums became more important than singles, bringing in more money. Record racks in department stores carried 100 albums, but only the top 40 singles. This gave the rack jobbers a chance to manipulate the charts.

The introduction of eight-track cartridges and compact cassettes gave companies a chance to recycle their backlists. General Recording Tape paid $75 million for the exclusive rights to duplicate RCA's catalogue for five years, starting in 1972.

Even mainstream radio had taken to rock. Revenues reached $1.4 billion in 1971 and doubled over the decade. Extensive tours promoted new albums, though the labels deducted tour expenses from record sales, so that only very big names like the Rolling Stones made money from them. The Stones had the clout to demand 90 per cent of their tours' gross takings but Atlantic could make that back from sales of the Stones' back catalogue that tours would generate.

GIANT SQUEEZE

The major labels also began to buy up the smaller ones, which gave them more control over the artists. CBS/Columbia had Epic, Philadelphia International, Portrait, Unlimited Gold, Tabu, Blue Sky, City Lights, Life-song, Jet Kirschner, Nemperor and Caribou. EMI had EMI (America), Capitol, United Artists, Seraphim, Harvest, Angel and Blue Note. MCA had Source and Motown. RCA had Arista, Bluebird, Rocket, Grunt, Wingsong and Different Drummer.

Warner, who came into the running on the back of rock and roll, had diversified into WEA — Warner-Elektra-Atlantic. They had Warner Records, Warner-Spector, Warner-Curb, Elektra/Asylum, Elektra/Curb, Atlantic, Atco, Rolling Stones Records and Swan Song, along with Dark Horse, Island, Sire, Bearsville, Nonesuch, Big Tree and Cotillion.

The American majors, no longer content to license acts from England, opened offices in London and across Europe. CBS celebrated total sales of $362.5 million and a net profit of $25 million in 1973. WEA turned over $235.9 million, yielding a profit of $22.2 million the same year. And Capitol netted $5.2 million from sales of $142.3 million.

By 1975 record and tape sales had leapt to $2.36 billion, nearly doubling since the beginning of the decade. The major contribution came from super-bands left over from the sixties. The Rolling Stones grossed $13 million from their 1975 tour and Bob Dylan and The Who did almost as well.

Sales for the record industry as a whole topped $4 billion in the year 1978. WEA grossed a healthy $600 million, but PolyGram sold 28 million copies of just one album, the Bee Gees's *Saturday Night Fever,* and turned over $1.6 billion. The record industry seemed to be riding high. In fact, it was riding for a fall — the so-called "Crash of '79".

THE DISCO CRAZE

By the mid-1970s, the sixties supergroups were entering middle age. They were hugely wealthy and out of touch with street sounds. Their music became over-produced and pompous. And, although it still reflected the tastes of the baby-boomers, it had little to say to the working-class teenagers who dominate the record-buying market.

In 1976 bands like the Ramones in the United States and the Sex Pistols in Great Britain started the punk revolution. It was a direct assault on the prevailing pop culture and a wave of new bands spawned a flock of new labels.

The majors, however, concentrated on disco. Its synthetic sound depended more on electronics and production than on star-quality; so it gave record companies even more power over their artists. Suddenly the disco craze was over and the majors found that they had no new talent to put in its place. And recession and double-digit inflation were destroying the consumers' purchasing power.

Record sales dropped from $4.2 billion in 1978 to $3.6 billion in 1979. The number of gold albums, which sold over half a million copies, dropped from 193 to 112. And platinum albums, those selling more than a million, dropped from 112 to 42.

Without the 30-million sellers, PolyGram found it was not shipping enough product to justify its huge distribution system. Companies found that they could not recoup the huge advances they had paid out for signings. Nor could they afford the massive sums that they handed over to independent record-promoters. MCA laid off 300 employees. Even the giant corporation, CBS, found that it had to cut its staff to the bone.

CBS

ABOVE: **Columbia was not always an equal-opportunities employer, but by the seventies overt racial discrimination had all but disappeared in the music industry.**

The CBS record label is a division of the Columbia Broadcasting System, based in New York, and a descendant of the oldest record label in the world, Columbia. By the early 1920s Columbia had become a British company which began reinvesting back in the United States. It put some money into radio and set up the Columbia Phonograph Broadcasting System. It was unprofitable and Columbia pulled out. But the network survived. It dropped the "phonograph" from its name and became CBS.

In 1938 CBS itself moved into the record industry, buying Brunswick Records who, by then, owned the rights to the Columbia name in the United States. EMI owned the name in the rest of the world. But Brunswick was not doing well. Of 33 million records sold in the United States in 1938, only seven million came from Brunswick. So CBS stripped it of the Columbia name and sold Brunswick to Decca in 1942.

"Big Red" hits the top

CBS changed Columbia's black label to the "Big Red" (it has since reverted) and spent $700,000 buying some of the best recordings of Louis Armstrong, Duke Ellington and Bessie Smith. They signed stars like Count Basie and Benny Goodman and halved the price of records to stimulate sales. Soon Columbia was the label with the biggest turnover in the United States.

CBS introduced the LP in 1948 and began to dominate the American market. Paul Weston, Mitch Miller and Percy Faith were staff A&R men. The jazz roster had Thelonious Monk, Dave Brubeck and Miles Davis. The pop roster included Johnny Mathis, Rosemary Clooney and Guy Mitchell. And the company had a string of hits with Broadway musicals and film soundtrack albums.

OPPOSITE: **Michael Jackson became the world's number-one selling artist with Quincy Jones at Epic, under the Columbia—CBS umbrella. Almost single-handedly, he turned loss into massive profit.**

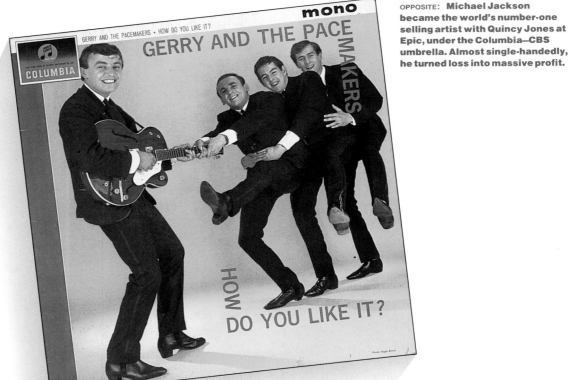

RIGHT: **Gerry and the Pacemakers were one of EMI's early Merseybeat signings to Parlophone. They had three number ones in the UK with their first three releases. In the post-Beatles scramble to sign up British acts, Columbia grabbed Gerry and his band.**

MAVERICKS IN THE BUSINESS I:

Clive Davis

Clive Davis, the man who took Columbia into the rock age, was pushed out in a boardroom tussle and then went on to make a huge success of another label, Arista.

Davis joined CBS as a lawyer in 1960. By 1966 he had worked his way up to the position of vice-president and general manager of the largest record company in the United States. At that time, Columbia's pop output consisted largely of original-cast albums from Broadway shows and records by middle-of-the-road crooners like Tony Bennett and Andy Williams. Bob Dylan was the label's only contemporary artist. RCA had Elvis Presley and Capitol had the Beatles. Suddenly these two smaller companies were challenging the giant.

Davis changed all that. His first signing was Great Britain's answer to Bob Dylan, the folk-rocker, Donovan. Then he went to the 1967 Monterey Pop Festival, where he snapped up Blood, Sweat and Tears and Janis Joplin. He signed Santana, Chicago, Johnny and Edgar Winter, Neil Diamond, Billy Joel and Bruce Springsteen and he managed to hold on to Bob Dylan at a time when Dylan seemed determined to change record labels.

But Columbia had a powerful old guard who resented the changes Davis had wrought. In the economic recession of 1973, the company found itself overextended and Davis carried the can. He was accused of fiddling his expenses and sacked. Subsequently, he cleared his name of the charges.

A year later after the sacking, Columbia Pictures called him in to run its Bell label. He used it to introduce the Kinks to the United States and to launch the career or Barry Manilow. And Dionne Warwick and Aretha Franklin revived their flagging careers at Arista.

Bertelsmann bought the label in 1979, but under the new owners Arista did not turn in any profits and RCA bought 50 per cent. Then Davis discovered Whitney Houston. Bertelsmann bought RCA and took Arista back into its American fold.

RIGHT: Columbia boss Clive Davis was fired, told all in an autobiography, then resurfaced at Columbia Pictures' ailing Bell label, which Davis renamed Arista.

OPPOSITE FAR RIGHT: Janis Joplin was one of Davis's first signings after his rock-and-roll conversion. She offered to sleep with him to clinch the deal.

OPPOSITE RIGHT BOTTOM: When it came to the English invasion, Davis was no slouch. He grabbed British folk-rocker Donovan, who was billed, inaccurately, as Britain's answer to Bob Dylan.

BELOW: After Davis signed them to Columbia, Chicago became one of rock's highest-earning groups. They were originally called the Chicago Transit Authority, but trimmed back their name after being sued by Chicago's Mayor Daley.

CBS

CBS

CBS

Clive Davis led CBS into the 1960s rock revolution. He signed a huge roster of rock artists and the company invested $7 million in Stax. But Stax did not produce the goods. It had Aretha Franklin, but lost her to Atlantic. The company's venture into black music eventually yielded dividends with Philadelphia International – Philly – giving them the O'Jays, Billy Paul and Harold Melvin and the Blue Notes. Davis, however, was pushed out and his protégé, Walter Yetnikoff, took over.

Yetnikoff immediately rallied his forces by declaring war on Warner Brothers. Bruce Springsteen came to CBS, as did Michael Jackson, but despite these artists' huge success, the wild antics of drug-crazed rock stars and the record industry's links to organized crime did not sit well with a conservative corporation like CBS, which depended on federal licences to continue their main business, broadcasting.

CBS had switched its European leasing from EMI to Philips in the early 1950s. In the late 1960s it began to use the CBS label to market Columbia's product outside the United States. Since then it has been repeatedly rumoured that CBS would drop the old Columbia name for the CBS label in the United States as well as internationally. In the 1980s it tried to buy the overseas rights to the Columbia name from EMI. EMI was willing to sell the name, since it was scarcely using the Columbia label in Great Britain. But each EMI subsidiary around the world owned a piece of the name and the deal collapsed.

For the parent company, this was the final straw. CBS tried to rid itself of CBS Records by reversing the deal and selling its music interests to EMI. But Walter Yetnikoff put in a bid with the Japanese giant, Sony, who eventually bought CBS Records for $2 billion.

OPPOSITE: **The Boss, Bruce Springsteen, came to Columbia in the early seventies, but it was not until the early eighties that he began to clock up the hits.**

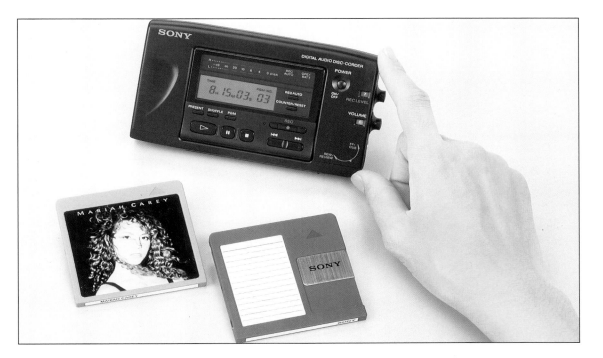

RIGHT: **After losing out over Betamax, Sony took over Columbia to help launch compact discs. And they have still newer formats to offer the world's music-buying public.**

MAVERICKS IN THE BUSINESS II:

Walter Yetnikoff

Since May, 1975, when he became head of CBS Records, Walter Yetnikoff has been the most powerful man in the record industry.

The son of a Jewish tailor, he was brought up in Brooklyn. Against his father's advice, he put himself through law school. He was shy and a little rough around the edges when his law firm sent him to a party at CBS Records, around Christmas time, in 1961. Yetnikoff was impressed and about a week later the up-and-coming Clive Davis offered Yetnikoff a job as his assistant. The offer was accepted.

When Davis became president of the label, he gave Yetnikoff the international division. Yetnikoff quickly fitted into Davis's rock-orientated company, abandoning his old suits, buying Chelsea boots and growing his sideburns. When Davis fell from grace, CBS Records found itself under the awkward stewardship of Irwin Segelstein, brought in from the company's TV division. Two years later Yetnikoff took over as president.

Yetnikoff quickly made his presence felt. He declared war on Warner Brothers, who were known in the company as the "communists".

He threw off his reputation for being shy and self-effacing and rocked the industry with his abrasive manner. His tantrums were legendary. He threatened to hound rival label bosses out of the industry when they signed acts he wanted. When Davis came back into the business as head of Arista, Yetnikoff threatened to punch him on the nose. He even threatened Richard Branson with financial extinction in 1984, over a matter so trivial tthat it was soon forgotten.

Yetnikoff was known for his explosive mixture of scatalogical and Yiddish expletives: he referred to PolyGram as Nazis. This did not sit well with William Paley, CBS's founder, an assimilated Jew. And Yetnikoff got on even less well with Paley's successor, Larry Tisch.

At the time, CBS Records was becoming embroiled in a scandal over the connections between record promoters and organized crime, and CBS wanted rid of its troublesome record division. Sony were looking for a record company. Yetnikoff negotiated the sale, and stayed on, more powerful than ever, as head of Columbia.

WARNER BROTHERS

Warner Brothers' first move into the record business was a disaster. Although the company's huge success in the movies proved that it knew something about public taste, it knew nothing about the music industry. In 1930 it bought Brunswick and four leading music publishers. But the Depression had killed record sales and the publishers had still not resolved the dispute with the radio stations over broadcasting royalties. Even though they commanded the work of Richard Rodgers, Jerome Kern, George Gershwin and Cole Porter, Brunswick and the publishing ventures proved insufficiently profitable and were sold off.

Warner Brothers had another try in 1958, with their own label. This time they recorded talent they knew – movie stars like Tab Hunter. But from 1958 to 1962 they lost an estimated $3 million a year.

The film company was about to close down its music division yet again, even at the risk of losing money owed to them by slow-paying distributors. Then Warner suddenly made progress: deviating from its movie-star policy, it signed the Everly Brothers, who gave the label its first number one with "Cathy's Clown". It was the Everlys' biggest hit, spending five weeks at the top of the American charts.

The folk trio, Peter, Paul and Mary, was the label's next successful signing and the company began to develop the takeover as its main commercial weapon. It bought Reprise from Frank Sinatra in 1963,

OPPOSITE: **Prince first went into the studio in his home town of Minneapolis. He took his demo to the New York labels, with no success. But a trip to Los Angeles brought a long-term contract with Warner Brothers and personal control of the label's subsidiary, Paisley Park Records.**

BELOW: **Ben E. King spent most of his prolific career at Atlantic, first with the Drifters, then – at the company's suggestion – developing as a solo act. He left Atlantic at the end of the sixties but returned after unsuccessful spells at Mandala and Maxwell-Crewe. In 1968, the Atco label came under Warners' wing as part of the Atlantic buy-out.**

WARNER BROTHERS

LEFT: Captain Beefheart released his first single on A&M, but soon started changing record label as frequently as other people change their socks. At Warner Brothers, he produced "Shiney Beast Bat Chain Puller".

ABOVE: Prolific singer-songwriter Joni Mitchell began her career on Reprise, but moved on to Asylum in 1972. Then, in 1982, she followed her former manager Dave Geffen on to the Geffen label, where she revived her flagging career.

thereby gaining middle-of-the-road hits with Trini Lopez, Dean Martin and Nancy Sinatra. In 1968 Atlantic and its labels, Atco and Cotillion, fell into the Warner Brothers fold. And when Elektra/Asylum was added in 1970, the group was renamed WEA – Warner Elektra Atlantic.

Warner Brothers had James Taylor and signed Ry Cooder before his first album. WEA (UK) paid for itself by signing Fleetwood Mac and Reprise licensed the Kinks and Petula Clark. Reprise's American talent included Neil Young, Joni Mitchell and Kenny Rogers. And on the more radical front, WEA had Captain Beefheart.

WEA's takeover strategy was thwarted in the 1980s by an anti-trust suit which prevented its merger with PolyGram. But links with Paisley Park gave it Prince and Sire produced Madonna. The group also signed Laurie Anderson, the Cars and Van Halen. Talking Heads, Anita Baker and Tracy Chapman were also introduced by Warner. Like other major record companies, the label is kept going through times when short-lived rock and pop talents fail by country music. WEA have Randy Travis, Hank Williams and Emmylou Harris.

ELEKTRA/ASYLUM
AND THE DAVE GEFFEN LABEL

Elektra had been started in New York City by Jac Holzman. Even with talent like Sonny Terry and Brownie McGhee, it was five years before he could pay himself a salary — and then only $100 a week.

In 1956 Elektra broke even. By 1963 it was a giant among independent labels. It had Judy Collins and Phil Ochs, and Dylan had made their brand of folk-rock very fashionable. In 1970 Holzman sold the company that he had started with $600 for the sum of $6.8 million to Warner Brothers.

The rock "wonder boy", Dave Geffen, did even better. He started Asylum Records in 1972 with money he had made from the sale of some publishing interests to CBS and signed Jackson Browne, Linda Ronstadt, Joni Mitchell and the Eagles. A year later he sold Asylum to Warner Communications for $7 mililion and, in 1973, became head of Warner's merged Elektra/Asylum group. His remarkable rise to prominence is detailed below.

Rise of the "Wonder Boy"

The Geffen label was named for its founder, David Geffen. It was not the first record label that Geffen founded. He had started Asylum in 1970. His forays into the music business have made him one of the Forbes "Four Hundred", *Forbes* magazine's list of the four hundred richest Americans. He is estimated to be worth $500 million.

Geffen started in show business as the postboy at the William Morris Agency. He later moved to the Ashley Famous agency, where

ABOVE: **Emerging from the underground, the Doors were signed by Elektra in 1966. Since the death of Jim Morrison in 1971 and the subsequent break-up of the band, the Doors have steadily increased their influence and mythic status — not to mention record sales.**

LEFT: **Jackson Browne was Asylum's first artist. His manager Dave Geffen could not secure him a recording contract — not even with Atlantic — so launched Asylum in order to release his 1971 album, *Saturate Before Using*.**

ELEKTRA/ASYLUM

ELEKTRA/ASYLUM

he handled the current crop of pop musicians. He quit to manage the singer and song-writer, Laura Nyro, and he formed a publishing company to handle her output.

Geffen took Nyro to Columbia, who signed her. Her albums did not do well, but her songs did sell well for other CBS artists – Three Dog Night, Fifth Dimension and Barbara Streisand and Blood, Sweat and Tears. This gave Geffen the opportunity to sell Nyro's publishing company to CBS for $4.5 million of stock. He kept half.

Next, he managed Crosby, Stills and Nash. To put the group together, he had to negotiate with the three separate labels to whom their current bands were contracted. When he asked Atlantic to free Steven Stills from his Buffalo Springfield obligations, Jerry Wexler had him thrown out of the door. But Ahmet Ertegun called him back the next day, released Stills and signed the new band to Atlantic.

Geffen merged his management company with Eliot Roberts, who managed Joni Mitchell. They discovered Jackson Browne, but could not find a record label to take him. So Geffen and Roberts set up one themselves – Asylum.

Delivering the goods

Asylum soon added Joni Mitchell, the Eagles and Linda Ronstadt. After a year, Geffen sold Asylum to Warner for $7 million, but remained president. And when Elektra's founder, Jac Holzman, retired, he took over Elektra, too. Warner was delighted because Geffen delivered the goods. He signed Tom Waits the re-formed Byrds – and he coaxed Bob Dylan from CBS for two albums.

Geffen was promoted to the Warner Brother ladder to vice-chairman of the movie company, leaving Asylum and Elektra in the hands of Joe Smith. In 1976 Geffen was diagnosed with cancer. As a result, he quit Warner. Four years later, it turned out that he did not have cancer after all.

In 1980 he started the Geffen label, buying in Donna Summer and Elton John for huge fees. They did not earn their keep. A third signing, John Lennon, did. Lennon's shaky comeback album, *Double Fantasy*, did not sell well at first; but when Lennon was gunned down outside the Dakota Building in New York in December, 1980, Geffen found he could not press enough copies of the album. It sold three million.

Geffen Records signed Asia, Neil Young, Peter Gabriel and Was Not Was. Then, at the end of the 1980s, Geffen, hit heavy-metal paydirt with megabands like Whitesnake and Guns 'N' Roses. They helped double the label's turnover in just two years to some $175 million.

OPPOSITE: **Tom Waits moved from cult cabaret artist to stardom with a carefully constructed career at Elektra and Asylum. But in 1983, he switched to Island where he produced three more albums.**

TOP RIGHT: **Disco diva Donna Summer began singing professionally in the German production of *Hair*. In Germany, she recorded the quasi-orgasmic "Love to Love You Baby". Casablanca picked it up in the US and she cranked out a series of disco hits for them. Geffen bought her in when Casablanca failed.**

RIGHT: **MCA broke Elton John in the US. Dave Geffen bought him to the Geffen label in 1982. But after two albums – *The Fox* and *Jump Up* – John returned to MCA.**

ISLAND

Although Island was founded on 8 May, 1962 in London, its story began on the island of Jamaica. It was there that Chris Blackwell had heard Lance Hayward, a blind Bermudian pianist, and his jazz combo and decided to record them — and start his own label. He called it Island after the 1957 novel, *Island in the Sun,* by Alec Waugh, which later became a film. He incorporated his new label for just $100.

His first album, *Lance Hayward At The Half Moon,* released a few weeks later, was not a success. But in 1960 he had his first hit with an R&B single by Laurel Aitken called "Little Sheila" with "Boogie In My Bones" on the flip side. It went to number one.

Blackwell's next release went to number one, too, and by the spring of 1962 he had opened an office in Kingston as a fully fledged record-producer. But Blackwell was up against fierce local competition from producers like Sir Coxone Dodd, Duke Reid and King Edwards. He soon found that he was selling more in Great Britain than in Jamaica and he decided to move there.

One-man operation

When Island Records was established in Great Britain, it was a one-man operation. For two years Blackwell's home was his office. He even handled the distribution himself. He kept his stock in the back of his blue Mini-Cooper and delivered to the shops in person. None of his records was a hit, but his releases of Jamaican dance tunes found a dedicated specialist market in the black areas of London and the big cities of the North.

One of the first singles Island released was "We'll Meet" by Roy and Millie. Impressed with Millie's infectious vocal, Blackwell brought the 15-year-old singer to England. She covered a single that Blackwell had bought in New York six years before called "My Boy Lollipop". It sold six million copies worldwide.

OPPOSITE: **At home in the islands, Chris Blackwell became the champion of Caribbean and Third World music. Once he had established the Island sound in Britain, he found it had a ready audience in the US too.**

ISLAND

TOP: **Island was instrumental in bringing the sound of Jamaica — rock steady and reggae — to Britain, then the world. Its founder Chris Blackwell, loved good music first and foremost, and tried to bring it to a wider audience.**

ABOVE: **Spencer Davis with an old two-track tape recorder — not the equipment he used as a producer and publicist at Island in the 1970s.**

ABOVE: **Island remembers its origins in its logo. Inside the "i" there is a palm tree. The "i" also stands for independent: not only has Island been one of the world's most successful independent labels, it has encouraged other small concerns to get off the ground.**

LEFT: **Island also built up an impressive rock list. Its success owes a lot to the fact that Blackwell spotted, long before the majors, that the record-buying public was moving towards albums and away from singles.**

MAVERICKS IN THE BUSINESS III:

Chris Blackwell

Chris Blackwell was born in London just before the outbreak of the Second World War. His father was Irish, his mother, Blanche Lindo, the daughter of an old Jamaican trading family.

At the age of six months, Blackwell was taken to Jamaica. When he was 10 he returned to England to go to school; he went back to Jamaica in 1955 when his formal education was over and became the aide-de-camp of the Governor General of Jamaica, Sir Hugh Foot. Later, he sold real estate and hired out motor scooters. Then, in 1959, his love of music took him to New York, where he spent six months hanging out on the jazz circuit, befriending Miles Davis.

Back in Jamaica, Blackwell heard a jazz combo, led by the blind Bermudan pianist, Lance Hayward, and decided to record them.

ISLAND

Blackwell took on six staff and went on tour with Millie. In a small Birmingham club he heard the Spencer Davis Group with its 15-year-old lead singer, Steve Winwood, and signed them.

He quickly realized that Spencer Davis was going to be too big for him to handle and he licensed the band to Philips. After three hits – "Keep on Running", "Gimme Some Lovin'" and "I'm A Man" – the Spencer Davis Group broke up. Steve Winwood went on to form Traffic – Island's first rock band – and his older brother, Muff Winwood, Spencer Davis's bassist, became an A&R man and producer. He later moved to CBS. And after two more incarnations of the Spencer Davis Group, Davis himself joined Island as an executive.

By the end of the sixties, Island had broadened its rock list to include Mott the Hoople, King Crimson, Free, Spooky Tooth, Emerson Lake & Palmer, Quintessence, Cat Stevens and Jethro Tull.

Island pushed albums rather than singles, outflanking the majors. Jethro Tull's young management team, Chris Wright and Terry Ellis,

ABOVE: **It was Island's development of Bob Marley and the Wailers that established reggae as a major force. The company followed up with a long list of reggae discoveries.**

ISLAND

LEFT: **Toots and the Maytals had a 12-year career in Jamaica before winning their first major recording deal with Island in 1975. That same year they broke into the American market.**

BELOW: **The smooth sound of Roxy Music had been rejected by most British record companies when Island took a chance in 1972. They immediately had a hit with "Virgin Plain", and Atlantic took them on in the US. But in 1977 Roxy Music quit Island and Atlantic for Polydor.**

joined Island. But Blackwell encouraged them to form their own label, Chrysalis, which was distributed by Island until the mid-seventies.

Island made the running in English folk-rock, too, when American Joe Boyd's Witchseason Productions brought Fairport Convention, Sandy Denny, Richard and Linda Thompson, John Martyn and Nick Drake to the label. The label's success made its Notting Hill studio one of the most sought-after recording facilities in the world.

Blackwell's greatest discovery

But Island Records was to score even greater successes by returning to its roots. Blackwell invested in the classic Jamaican film, *The Harder They Come,* and pushed Island star, Jimmy Cliff, into the leading role. That same year Blackwell met his greatest discovery, Bob Marley.

Marley walked into Blackwell's London office penniless. He had been touring with Johnny Nash, had been stranded in Sweden and did not have money to get back to Jamaica. Blackwell signed him immediately and produced most of Marley's albums in an era when most record-company executives could not find their way around a studio.

The success of Bob Marley put reggae on the world stage. Island added to its reggae list by signing Burning Spear, Third World, Toots and the Maytals, Lee Perry, Inner Circle and Sly and Robbie. It even opened a studio in Nassau called Compass Point. The house band, the Compass Point Allstars, included Sly Dunbar, Robbie Shakespeare, Barry Reynolds, Mikey Chung, Wally Badarou and Sticky Thompson. They were instrumental in creating the distinctive sound of Grace Jones's early albums for Island.

While it was Island that made reggae a world force, the label kept up in other areas of rock by signing Robert Palmer, Sparks, Eddie & the Hot Rods, John Cale, Kevin Ayers, Hi-Tension, Roxy Music and the then little-known U2.

As well as helping Chysalis get off the ground, Island distributed Virgin until 1976. It was also associated with the punk label Stiff and ZTT, who produced Frankie Goes to Hollywood.

In 1988 Island signed a deal with the fledgling Los Angeles rap label, Delicious Vinyl, that took Tone Loc's "Wild Thing" to the top of the American charts in 1989.

Island has expanded into the world of movies, producing *Kiss of the Spiderwoman* and *The Trip to the Bountiful.* But the core business – producing records – has not been forgotten. Three sister labels have been launched: Mango, which handles Third World music, Antilles for jazz and fusion, and Fourth & Broadway for dance and black music.

Island signed The Christians, whose near-million-selling first album was the biggest-selling debut album in Island's history. Julian Cope had a hit single with "World Shut Your Mouth". Courtney Pine became the only serious jazz musician to make a recent Top 40 album. And Africa's rising star, Salif Keita, has signed to Mango.

STIFF

S tiff Records was the archetypal punk label. The name "stiff" itself is pure punk – record-industry slang for a real turkey, a record that had no hope.

Although punk's early influences – Iggy Pop and the Ramones – came from the United States, Stiff was formed in London in July, 1976, by Andrew "Jake" Jakeman and David Robinson.

Jakeman had been tour manager with Dr Feelgood in the United States. He had noticed that everywhere he went there were small town record labels who recorded local talent. Selling through neighbourhood stores, a label could have a local hit; and airplay on local radio station meant that a record could be picked up by one of the majors and become a "regional breakout".

Back in England, Jakeman met up with Robinson, who ran a studio at a London pub and had recorded every band that played there between 1973 and 1975. He had amassed a large library of live tapes.

A shoestring operation

Jakeman and Robinson picked a handful of neglected artists, including Nick Lowe, Motorhead, Dave Edmunds and Graham Parker. Jakeman borrowed £400 from Lee Brilleaux of Dr Feelgood and the Stiff record label was born. Early Stiff records were sold by mail order, from the backs of trucks and through a few small record shops.

In 1976 punk was happening in pubs and clubs and on the streets of London. It had caught the imagination of the press, but there were no punk records to buy.

Stiff signed The Damned, Wreckless Eric and Elvis Costello – the "Elvis" was Jakeman's idea. Soon the label was swept along in punk's tide. By July, 1977, it was selling so well that a distribution deal was signed with Island, which was, in turn, distributed by EMI. When EMI ran into financial trouble, Stiff turned to CBS for distribution.

In September, 1977, Jakeman split, taking Elvis Costello, Nick Lowe and the Yachts to the newly formed Radar Records, and it was assumed that Stiff was dead. But Island was understanding and a major push on Ian Dury kept the label alive.

The signing of Lena Lovich, Madness and the Belle Stars carried the label's early fortunes into the 1980s. In its first six years it released 150 singles, with over 30 per cent of them making the charts. That is as good an average as any of the majors can boast.

OPPOSITE: **Iggy Pop's seminal work with the Stooges kept cropping up in the New Wave repertoire. Without the self-styled godfather of punk, Stiff Records might never have been formed.**

RIGHT: **Under Stiff's chaotic management, the Damned became the first British punk band to record, make the charts and to tour America. They signed with Stiff in September 1976 and released "New Rose"/"Help" in October. Their album *Damned, Damned, Damned* followed in February 1977, while the Sex Pistols were still being dropped from contracts.**

OPPOSITE: **Elvis Costello was signed to Stiff under his real name Declan McManus. He left to join Stiff founder Andrew Jakeman at Radar Records, then moved to Jakeman's F-Beat label when Radar foundered. In the US, Costello was signed with Columbia.** INSET: **The Stiff label quips that the songs are "electrically recorded" and boasts that Stiff is "the world's most flexible record label". As well as performing, Nick Lowe produced all Stiff's early records.**

STIFF RECORDS

Recorded

Electrically

The worlds most flexible record label

LAST 1
LIVE SIDE

℗ & © 1977 Stiff
Records Ltd

*Shapiro/Bernstein
& Co Ltd
†Rock Music Co

SWAN STEREO

*1. BORN A WOMAN (2.30)
(Martha Sharp)
†2. SHAKE THAT
RAT (2.00)
(Nick Lowe)

Produced by
NICK LOWE
for Himself

NICK
LOWE

ALL RIGHTS OF THE RECORD PRODUCER AND OF THIS WORK REPRODUCED RESERVED COPYING, PUBLIC PERFORMANCE & BROADCASTING OF THIS RECORD PROHIBITED

 # THE EIGHTIES

The record industry entered the 1980s in poor shape. The Crash of '79 had cost it dear. At CBS Records, Dick Asher was called in as deputy-president to sort out the mess. He had the far from pleasant task of examining the books. In 1979 CBS's profits had dropped by 46 per cent and the company made just $51 million on a turnover of over $1 billion. Asher's eye was drawn to the biggest outlay on the balance sheet after salaries — the hundreds of millions that were being squandered on independent record-pluggers.

Asher had been in London during the 1970s, running CBS subsidiary there. When he had left the United States in 1972, a freelance promoter got about $100 a week. By 1980 it cost something like $100,000 to get an independent promoter to plug just one song.

The big promoters could guarantee you airplay, the vital exposure needed for a record to climb the charts. And you had to get the single into the charts to sell the album. If you did not pay the promoters, you got no airplay, no hit and no album sales.

THE "NETWORK"

The record companies were terrified of the word "payola". The payola scandal of the late 1950s had destroyed rock-and-roll DJ, Alan Freed, and badly damaged the industry. Keeping promotion at arm's length — with any bribes to DJs coming from independent promoters, not directly from the record companies — was very convenient.

But the promoters were organized. Each member of the so-called "Network" controlled its own turf. Each had its own stations that could "deliver" on demand. And the turf was not necessarily local. An "indie" in New Jersey could deliver airplay on stations in Detroit and Los Angeles. But you would have to deal with other members of the Network if you wanted airplays on other stations and there was growing evidence that the Network had ties with the Mafia, in particular the Gambino family.

Asher tried an experiment with Pink Floyd's *Wall* album. Floyd had always been an album band whose followers did not listen to Top 40 radio and Asher refused to pay out on the group's single, "Another Brick in the Wall". The "indies" kept it off Top 40 radio, but the album was promoted by a Pink Floyd tour and proved to be a huge success. Asher had proved his point: you could sell records without paying the "indies". He proposed a boycott of the independent promoters. CBS agreed and Warner joined in.

The Network struck back by pulling the airplay on a single by a group called Loverboy, signed by Asher to CBS Canada. It disappeared without trace. The Network went on to destroy The Who's single, "You Better You Bet", badly damaging sales of the album, *Face Dances.*

Two other British acts just breaking into the American market — the Boomtown Rats, with lead singer Bob Geldof, and Adam Ant — saw the dangers. They hired an attorney, Paul Marshall, to fight the ban. Marshall argued that, although the boycott of the independent promoters might be a moral issue for the record companies, for his clients, who were likely to have only a brief career, it was make or break. He bypassed Asher and went directly to CBS president, Walter Yetnikoff, who found a way to pay artists extra to employ their own independent pluggers. The boycott collapsed and Asher was pushed out of CBS.

THE CD REVOLUTION

At the same time, the rise of Michael Jackson and new artists like Whitney Houston began to turn the record industry round. Then, the arrival of the compact disc put profits back on a firm footing. Like compact cassettes before them, CDs offered record companies a way to recycle their backlists.

The Dutch company, Philips, part-owner of Poly-Gram, had first developed the technology and it signed a licensing agreement with Warners as a prelude to a takeover bid. CDs were taken up by Japanese electronics manufacturers, including Sony, who also developed DAT, a new tape format which applied CD's digital technology to cassette tape.

Philips had already established its position in the music market with the growing empire of Poly-Gram. Sony needed a record company with a huge back catalogue to guarantee the success of DAT. CBS was that company.

OPPOSITE: **By the early eighties, rap had become a serious commercial proposition. Originating in the mid seventies among black and Hispanic teenagers in New York City's outer boroughs, it combined chanting street poetry with a disco beat, breakdancing and graffiti art**

POLYGRAM

DEREK AND THE DOMINOS

Polydor

LAYLA
(Clapton-Gordon)
(from the L.P. "History of Eric Clapton")
2659-012)

PolyGram is another of the progeny of the gramophone inventor, Emile Berliner. It began as the German subsidiary of the Gramophone company which Berliner set up with his brothers, Jacob and Joseph, under the name, Deutsche Grammophon Gesellschaft.

DGG split form its British parent, HMV, during the First World War, when the German government seized DGG as enemy property. After the war EMI resolved the ownership battle by using DGG senior management to set up a new German subsidiary, Electrola. DGG, however, managed to retain the HMV trade mark, the dog Nipper, for use in Germany only. For export, DGG set up Polydor.

In 1940 the German electrical giant, Siemens, bought the company, but at the end of the Second World War DGG had to surrender the HMV trademark. It continued with the Polydor label, domestically and abroad, for pop music.

The other half of PolyGram was Phonogram, the recording label of the Dutch electrical giant, Philips. It was established in 1946 by Hans van Zoelen, a record-store owner who had been with Dutch Decca. In 1950 he sold out to Philips.

A 1952 licensing deal with CBS gave Philips/Phonograph the European distribution rights to some of the United States's best selling popular music output.

ABOVE: **The Platters – from left to right Herb Reed, Tony Williams, Zola Taylor, Paul Robi and Dave Lynch – first signed to Federal Records in 1953. In 1955, they moved to Mercury which was bought by Phonogram.**

In the 1960s Phonogram moved into the United States, buying the Mercury label, whose pop roster had been built up by Mitch Miller before he joined Columbia. This gave the label its first American number one – the Platters' "The Great Pretender".

In 1962 Siemens and Philips merged their music interests, Polydor and Phonogram. The result was PolyGram. The new company's early successes included the Walker Brothers, Dusty Springfield when she went solo, the Spencer Davis Group and Serge Gainsbourg and Jane Birkin's "Je T'aime".

In 1972 PolyGram went on a buying binge, purchasing Verve, MGM and the distribution operation of United Artists. But still the breakthrough it was after did not come. Based in Holland and Germany, the company did not understand the Anglo-American pop market. Their European stars sold well on the Continent, but a 13-year-old Dutch star like Hein Tje fell on deaf ears in Great Britain and the United States.

OPPOSITE: **The Bee Gees had made millions for Robert Stigwood's RSO label with the soundtrack of** *Saturday Night Fever.* **But they could not perform the same feat with the film of** *Sergeant Pepper's Lonely Hearts Club Band* **after PolyGram bought into RSO.**

POLYGRAM

Casablanca

The company, which was answerable to both the Siemens and the Philips boards, had more money than managerial sense. They invested further in the United States during the disco boom, buying into Neil Bogart's west coast label, Casablanca, which had the disco diva, Donna Summer. But Casablanca was awash with drugs and, though it turned out the hits, it was known in the business to "ship gold and return platinum". It hyped its hits and spent more in Mafia-controlled promotion than it could possibly make back in profit. PolyGram ended up losing millions.

PolyGram also bought into Robert Stigwood's RSO label, which had huge successes with the soundtrack albums from *Saturday Night Fever* and *Grease*. Then Stigwood produced a film version of the

Beatles' *Sergeant Pepper's Lonely Hearts Club Band* with the Bee Gees, Peter Frampton and George Burns. It bombed and PolyGram learned another expensive lesson.

But the label was big enough to cope with these setbacks. In 1980 it bought Decca UK and in 1983 it tried to merge with Warner Communications. The merger was blocked by American anti-trust laws. But in 1990 PolyGram managed to purchase Island and A&M for a combined total of $732 million.

PolyGram is one of only five major labels to have subsidiaries on all six continents, with record companies in over 18 countries. Only CBS and EMI are bigger. The parent company, Philips, developed the optical disc, the forerunner of the CD, and Philips and Sony built the first CD factory outside Japan in Hanover, on the site where DGG had begun gramophone technology in the 1890s.

LEFT: Although the LP *Sergeant Pepper's Lonely Hearts Club Band* made huge profits for EMI, Capitol and the Beatles, Robert Stigwood's soundtrack from the film of the same name taught PolyGram an expensive lesson.

MAVERICKS IN THE BUSINESS IV:

Dick Asher

Clive Davis brought Dick Asher to CBS in 1966. Asher had his own law practice when Davis, who was having problems at Columbia, turned to him for advice. They got on well and Davis persuaded Asher to join CBS as vice-president of business affairs.

Asher did well, but he felt that his contribution was overlooked after Davis was promoted to become president of Columbia in 1967. He quit in 1970 to head Capitol's East Coast division, but returned to Columbia the following year. Then he went to London as head of the UK division of CBS Records.

When Walter Yetnikoff took over as head of CBS Records, Yetnikoff recalled Dick Asher to New York and made him head of CBS International. But Asher and Yetnikoff fell out over the matter of the huge promotional budgets that seemed to be finding their way into the hands of organized crime. Asher was pushed out of CBS.

After nearly a year without work, Warner Communications called Asher in as a consultant on the Warner-PolyGram merger, then hired him full-time. When the merger fell through, he moved to PolyGram as its new head. He was lucky to take over just at the moment that the heavy-metal rockers, Bon Jovi, made their breakthrough. PolyGram also had Def Leppard, Scorpions and Rush – who all found a ready audience on MTV. Under Asher, PolyGram quickly moved into third position in the United States, behind CBS and Warner.

As the company expanded through its acquisition policy, Asher fell out with his European bosses. They were paying too much for the labels they were buying and the group was losing serious amounts of money in the United States. Meanwhile, his own salary skyrocketed to over a million dollars a year.

He was earning more than the head of Philips, PolyGram's parent company, and in November, 1989, the company had no option but to let him go.

ABOVE: **British heavy metal band Def Leppard did much better in America under Dick Asher's aegis at Mercury than they did in their own country.**

BELOW: **Bon Jovi were brought to PolyGram by Dick Asher. Along with Def Leppard, the Scorpions and Rush, Bon Jovi helped Asher make PolyGram the natural home of heavy metal.**

MCA

MCA — the Music Corporation of America — became a record label in the 1960s. But it had begun before the Second World War as a booking agency. Its founder, Jules Stein, had then got into management and movies with Paramount. MCA went into the record business by buying Decca's American subsidiary.

Decca had had a long and distinguished career in the United States. Louis Armstrong, Count Basie and Bing Crosby recorded on American Decca. By 1960 it had acquired Bill Haley, Peggy Lee and Buddy Holly and the Crickets on its Coral and Brunswick subsidiaries.

In the 1960s MCA got The Who from Great Britain and signed Ricky Nelson. It later signed the Pointer Sisters, Neil Diamond and Elton John. But the corporate plan remained expansion through acquisition — of Chess, Dunhill, ABC, ABC-Paramount, Westminster, Impulse, Dot, Bluesway and Command.

The "Poison Dwarf"

In 1974 MCA grouped everything together under its own MCA label, broke its ties with Decca UK and signed an agreement with EMI. But things did not go well. In the disco disaster of the later 1970s, MCA had to lay off 300 personnel. By 1983 its roster was reduced to Olivia Newton-John and a few country artists. The company cried out for new management. Columbia's Walter Yetnikoff was offered the job, but CBS upped Yetnikoff's salary — already $578,471 — and the former artists' manager, five-foot-three Irving Azoff — known even to his friends as "The Poison Dwarf" — took over as label boss.

TOP RIGHT: **MCA went into the record business by buying Decca US. Early records, including Jacki Wilson's "Soul Galore", were still manufactured in England by Decca UK.**

OPPOSITE: **Olivia Newton-John was a long-term profit-maker for MCA. She established herself in England with the help of Cliff Richard. But following MCA's release** Let Me Be There **in 1973, America became her main market.**

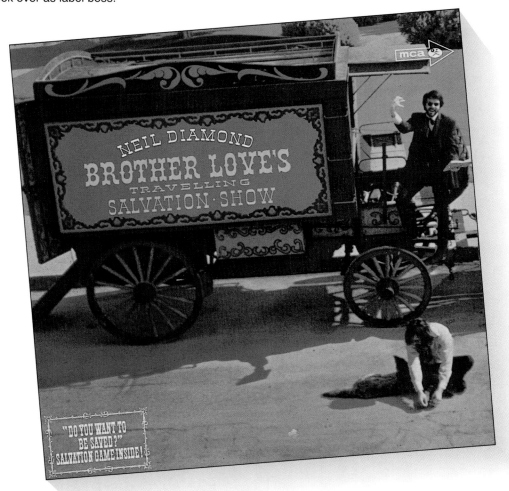

RIGHT: **Neil Diamond signed with MCA in 1968 to record** Touching You Touching Me. **Brother Love's Travelling Salvation Show in 1969 was the second of 15 albums Diamond made for MCA.**

MCA

MAVERICKS IN THE BUSINESS V:

Irving Azoff

Irving Azoff started in the music business as a booking agent in Dave Geffen's management firm. When Geffen left to set up Asylum, Geffen let him take the Eagles and form his own management company, Frontline. It became immensely successful, representing stars like Stevie Nicks, Don Henley, Steely Dan, Boz Scaggs and Jackson Browne.

Azoff's success stemmed from his extraordinary personality. He could meet, make friends and cut a deal in minutes. He could retain the details of hundreds of telephone conversations in his head. But when being nice didn't work, there was no bigger son of a bitch in the business. Azoff's tantrums were legend. He set fire to the menu in a Beverly Hills restaurant as a protest against the slow service. On another occasion, hotel staff had to restrain him from chucking a television out of a window to silence roadmenders in the street outside. He sent a live boa constrictor to rival manager, Michael Lippman, for his birthday. In a backhanded reference to Lippman's wife, the note accompanying the clinging snake said: "Happy birthday, Michael. Now you have two of them."

When Azoff took over MCA and sold his management interests to it, Dave Geffen pointed out the conflict of interest – two of MCA's stars found that they were now also managed by the company. Azoff dismissed Geffen and other critics as "crybabies".

RIGHT: **Don Henley was with Azoff's management company Frontline, but he and the Eagles followed Dave Geffen to Asylum. Henley later pursued his solo career on the Geffen label.**

MCA

LEFT: **In 1988, Azoff and MCA won the battle to buy out Motown. Lionel Richie came with the company and is still a bankable star.**

ABOVE: **Stevie Wonder was another of the artists that MCA acquired in their takeover of Motown. It could be argued that his backlist alone was worth the $61 million MCA paid for the company.**

Azoff quickly overhauled MCA – which some were calling the Music Cemetery of America at the time. One country artist and his manager had sued the company, alleging that MCA "were so inept they didn't legally constitute a record company". That manager was none other than Irving Azoff.

Azoff brought with him three management companies, which he sold to MCA in 1986 for $15.7 million. And on top of his $500,000 salary from MCA, he had interests in merchandising for rock acts.

But Azoff turned the company around. MCA outbid rivals for Motown, who still had Stevie Wonder and Lionel Richie. It had already attracted former Motown stars like Martha Reeves. MCA launched Tiffany, the teenage girl who sang in shopping malls, and she soon went platinum.

In 1989 Azoff moved on to WEA, where he launched a new label. His job went to Al Teller who, in March, 1990, bought the influential Geffen label for $545 million. Geffen Records was just 10 years old.

VIRGIN

he Virgin record label sprang from a mail-order record retail operation that Richard Branson began in 1969 to save his magazine, *The Student.* Branson began to buy records in bulk and sell them cut-price through ads in the magazine. The mail-order firm was named Virgin because Branson and his colleagues were cherries when it came to business.

The mail-order operation spawned the Virgin chain of record stores and a recording studio, The Manor, built in a country house in Oxfordshire. This was superintended by Branson's cousin, Simon Draper, and sound engineer, Tom Newman. Fairport Convention, Scaffold and Paul McCartney recorded there. And a young musician who stayed on after the studio's first paying customers, the Arthur Lewis Band, particularly impressed Branson. His name was Mike Oldfield, whose album *Tubular Bells* was to become a huge success and the launch-pad of Virgin's bright future.

Through the import department of Virgin's retail chain, Draper came across a number of Continental groups. Virgin signed Tangerine Dream from Germany and its album, *Phaedra,* gave the label another million seller. In 1974 Virgin moved to larger premises.

By 1975 Virgin's list of high-powered hippies was beginning to look a bit out of date. Attempts to sign 10cc, David Bowie, Pink Floyd,

The Who, even the Rolling Stones, were unsuccessful. Then punk happened. Branson and Draper flew to Ireland to try to sign Bob Geldof and the Boomtown Rats. But they signed with Ensign when Branson tried to take their music publishing, too.

Virgin began to take an interest in reggae and managed to sign Peter Tosh, who had sung with Bob Marley and the Wailers. *Legalize It* was issued in 1976, but much of Virgin's reggae output had to be off-loaded in Nigeria. Then the Sex Pistols happened.

In May, 1977, McLaren signed the Sex Pistols in time to issue the anti-monarchist "No Future" (more popularly known as "God Save the Queen") for Elizabeth II's silver jubilee. Though it was banned by the BBC, it sold 100,000 copies in the first week. Only some swift and dubious footwork by the British Market Research Bureau, who compile the British charts, prevented it from being number one in the week of the Jubilee celebrations. As the Sex Pistols broke up, relations between Branson and group manager Malcolm McLaren – never good – became strained. Eventually, Virgin took the future royalties of the now defunct Sex Pistols, the rights to McLaren's film *The Great Rock 'n' Roll Swindle* and signed Public Image Ltd (PIL), the new group formed by ex-Pistol John Lydon (aka Johnny Rotten). Salt was rubbed further into McLaren's wounds when he found that his American label, Charisma was bought out by his arch-rival Branson.

TUBULAR BELLS

In nine months, playing 28 instruments on 23,000 over-dubs, Oldfield produced an album called *Tubular Bells*. Branson created a record label, Virgin, and signed him. For distribution Branson went to Island Records, who, initially wanted a production deal with Virgin. It would have given Virgin a substantial advance and Island an 18 per cent royalty. Instead, Branson pushed for a distribution deal which would give Island only 10–15 per cent — but there would be no advance. This was a high-risk strategy for Branson. Unless he had a hit with one of his first few records, Virgin might sink forever.

Branson admitted he knew nothing about music, but he had confidence in his cousin, Simon Draper, Manor studio's technical wizz, Tom Newman, and Oldfield himself. He had to open negotiations with CBS before Island came round.

The gamble paid off. *Tubular Bells* went to number one in Great Britain. Branson flew to New York and secured a $750,000 advance from the head of Atlantic Records, Ahmet Ertegun, who immediately persuaded the film director, William Friedkin, to use it as the theme music for *The Exorcist*. *Tubular Bells* soon topped the album charts in the United States, too.

ABOVE: No one had ever heard anything like *Tubular Bells*, and the major companies all rejected it. But when it was finally released, it was greeted with huge critical acclaim and massive sales — making an extraordinary debut for Oldfield and for Virgin.

RIGHT: Richard Branson launched the Virgin record label in 1973 to release Mike Oldfield's *Tubular Bells*. By 1981, it had sold ten million copies. Oldfield made another 15 albums for Virgin.

LEFT: Virgin star Boy George shows off Culture Club's Ampex Golden Reel Award for *Kissing to be Clever* outside Red Bus Studios. Legend has it that Boy George waited in Virgin's reception, day in day out, until Branson finally let him record.

Despite the demise of the Sex Pistols, Virgin managed to refresh its lists with new wave bands like Magazine, Penetration, the Members and the Skids.

In 1978 Virgin opened a New York office in a brownstone in Greenwich Village. It failed, losing half a million pounds in the process, and Virgin moved into continental Europe, signing local acts in Italy, France and Germany.

Virgin moved into the 1980s with Human League, Japan, Heaven 17, Simple Minds and Phil Collins, paying an unprecedented £65,000 for a solo album by a drummer. But it was the huge success of Boy George that moved Virgin into the major leagues. It gave the company the money to move into movies, book publishing and open an airline. In 1987, Virgin moved into the United States again and had its first American number one with the English group, Cutting Crew.

In 1987, by then one of Great Britain's largest private companies, was floated on the stockmarket. It was a safe bet. As Branson pointed out, 40 per cent of its turnover came not from new releases, but from an extensive backlist, and 40 per cent came from the French artists, not from the likes of Boy George. But barely 18 months after the flotation, Branson bought back a controlling interest in the shares. The company became his again.

BELOW: The Virgin logo is one of the record industry's best-known corporate identities. It also appears on record stores, books, aeroplanes, movies and condoms.

VIRGIN

VIRGIN

HOW VIRGIN SIGNED
THE SEX PISTOLS

Signed to EMI by their svengali-like manager, Malcolm McLaren, the Sex Pistols appeared on TV on the afternoon of 1 December, 1976, and unleashed a torrent of obscenity. Branson immediately called EMI and offered to take them off EMI's hands. EMI agreed and McLaren promised to meet Branson later that day. Instead, he took £50,000 from EMI for the cancellation of the Sex Pistols contract and signed the group to A&M. After a party at A&M's London offices, where the Sex Pistols disgraced themselves less than a week after signing to the label, A&M gave them another £75,000 to go away. Ahead of the game to the tune of £125,000, the Sex Pistols still had no record company.

TOP: The Sex Pistols signed to Virgin for £50,000, after collecting £125,000 from EMI and A&M. Between them, these two labels had released just one of the band's singles, "Anarchy in the UK".

RIGHT: On his own admission, Richard Branson knows nothing about music. He leaves those decisions to others better qualified. What he lends to the Virgin label is his extraordinary nose for business opportunities.

LEFT: Phil Collins was another inspired Virgin signing. When it comes to solo careers, drummers usually need not apply. But Collins more than justified Virgin's unprecedented confidence.

ZTT

ZTT – Zang Tuum Tumb – was the brainchild of the ingenious producer, Trevor Horn. He and his partner, Geoffrey Downes, made their first appearance in the world of pop as the Buggles, whose "Video Killed the Radio Star" became a huge international hit in 1979. After a follow-up single, Horn and Downes joined Yes. They appeared on the supergroup's 1980 album, *Drama,* and played on its 1980–81 tour. Then Downes quit to join Asia. Horn stayed on as producer of the band's final album. He went on to produce ABC, Dollar and Malcolm McLaren's Duck Rock.

RIGHT: Holly Johnson was the only member of Frankie Goes to Hollywood to appear on the band's first two hit singles. After the band failed, ZTT took out an injunction against Johnson to try to prevent him going solo.

OPPOSITE: ABC was one of the bands produced by ZTT founder Trevor Horn. They had three top ten singles in the UK and a gold album after signing with Phonogram.

Frankie Goes to Hollywood

Horn formed ZTT in 1983 to launch the controversial Liverpudlian group, Frankie Goes To Hollywood. They had been turned down by Arista, but had found the money to produce a sado-masochistic promo-video for their song, "Relax". Horn signed them for a £500 advance, recorded the song and released it in October, 1983. Its sexually explicit lyrics – and the group's leather-clad homosexuality – quickly attracted attention. Success was assured when the BBC disc jockey, Mike Read, refused to play it. BBC TV also refused to air the video and the band took off.

Frankie Goes To Hollywood quickly followed up with "Two Tribes", which went straight to number one in Great Britain with "Relax" at number two – a feat previous achieved only by Elvis Presley, the Beatles and John Lennon. Their debut album *Welcome to the Pleasure Dome* went straight to the top fo the British album charts in 1984 and "The Power of Love" gave them a third consecutive hit single.

Frankie Goes To Hollywood went to Hollywood and broke into the United States in 1985. But success began to slip from their grasp. Their fourth single, "Rage Hard", did not do so well as the first three and their second album, *Liverpool '86,* was roasted by reviewers. Then the band broke up.

Horn tried to prevent Frankie's lead singer, Holly Johnson, from going solo. The court hearings revealed that – with the sole exception of Johnson – none of the band had played on their first two hits. Early versions of "Relax" had been made by Ian Dury's Blockheads. The impact of the records came largely from Horn's production. This revelation gave Horn the reputation of being a puppetmaster, in the glib mould of Stock, Aitken, Waterman.

ZTT continued with its other bands, Art of Noise and Propaganda. Horn's association with Island gave them Grace Jones' "Slave to the Rhythm". Seal is ZTT's latest star.

BELOW LEFT: ZTT produced the whole design package for their artists – image was as important as the music. With Frankie Goes to Hollywood, Horn took an eclectic approach, assembling cultural images as diverse as Ol' Blue Eyes, bondage and Lenin.

BELOW: Frankie Goes to Hollywood on stage managed to produce a unique mixture of menace and camp. Their demos of "Relax" and "Two Tribes" were rejected by Arista, but Trevor Horn bought them for an advance of just £5,000 and worked the ZTT magic on them.

THE NINETIES

Technology has led the way in the 1990s. CD has put PolyGram, Warner and sony in a commanding position. Sony even has its own pop label — Sony Soho Square, named after its London offices. It was established in July, 1991, under Muff Windwood, who has been with Columbia for over 13 years as Columbia's European label. So far it has managed to attract only British acts, including Des'ree, Naked Truth and the curiously named Ned's Atomic Dustbin.

Sony is now introducing another format, minidiscs, a smaller form of CD which can be recorded on as well as played.

Meanwhile the law has closed in in the United States. Independent promoters like Joe Isgro and Valerie Tashjian have been indicted for payola and racketeering. Morris Levy has been jailed. And Gambino godfather, John Gotti, who is also implicated in the independent promotion racket, has been sentenced to life imprisonment for murder and racketeering.

Black artists, always the backbone of the industry, are now standing up for themselves. The political stance of rap artists and the incredible success of MC Hammer for Capitol have made it difficult for managers and record companies to practise the same old rip-offs.

OPPOSITE: An increasingly vociferous moral lashback in the States has seen the rise of warning stickers on records (see picture on page 77) and demands for censorship. Madonna, Prince and 2LiveCrew (pictured) have all found themselves in trouble for the steamy sexuality of their songs.

DEF JAM

D ef Jam was founded in 1983 by "The King of Rap", Russell "Rush" Simmons, and Rick Rubin. Rap officially started four years before with the Sugarhill Gang's "Rapper's Delight", which reached number five in the R&B charts and number 40 on cross-over. By the early 1980s rap singles like Kurtis Blow's "The Breaks" were going gold.

Simmons is a middle-class New Yorker with a murky background in street politics and, allegedly, drug dealing. Whlie working as club promoter he met Kurtis Blow and became his manager. He formed Rush Artist Management in 1980. That led naturally to his forming his own record label, Def Jam. His feel for what was happening on the street and his natural business instinct enabled him to turn Def Jam and his Rush Group into one of the biggest African-American-owned companies in the United States.

Big-time rap

Among the first groups on the label were the first rap bands with number-one albums, the Beastie Boys, LL Cool J and Public Enemy. In 1985 Def Jam signed a label agreement with CBS Records. CBS had seen how profitable rap could be and in December, 1984, Run DMC gave the world the first gold rap album.

OPPOSITE: **LL Cool J was one of the first of the new breed of black artists to be signed to Def Jam. The label ensures that the profits stay in the black community, though Def Jam boss Russell Simmons is hapy to do distribution deals with the major white labels.**

BELOW: **The Beastie Boys on Def Jam and Run DMC on Profile showed how profitable the street-sound of rap could be. The Beastie Boys played it controversial and white, while Run DMC made rap accessible to a large white audience with their heavy-metal cross-overs.**

DEF JAM

Run DMC emerged on the small "indie" label, Profile Records, but it was one of Simmon's Rush Productions' groups, which also included Whodini, first rap Grammy winners, Jazzy Jeff and Fresh Prince, Stetsatonic, and Eric B. & Rakim. In 1986 Simmons moved into R&B, creating the OBR – Original Black Records – label. Its roster includes The Black Flames, Newkirk, Tashran and Alyson Williams.

In 1988 Rick Rubin left to start his own label. Simmons was then sole owner of the company. In 1991 he upgraded his arrangement with CBS Records – by then Sony Music – into a joint venture agreement. Def Jam's roster now includes Downtown Science, Nikki D, EPMD (who have gone multi-gold), 3rd Bass (multi-gold), Slick Rick (platinum), LL Cool J (multi-platinum) and Public Enemy (multi-platinum).

Simmons diversified with five so-called Rush Associated Labels. RAL is a joint venture with Sony Music. Run by Simmons and Lyor Cohen it aims to give street-smart producers their own labels and greater creative and financial control. RAL gives them a central administration and Sony Music handles marketing and distribution. Labels include Dew Doo Man Records. The president is Prince Paul, who had produced hits for De La Soul and 3rd Bass. His roster includes Resident Alien and Mic Tee Lux.

Fever Records was founded by Sal Abbatiello and Andy "Panda" Tripoli. It has been influential in Latin pop music since 1985. It has signed The Cover Girls and Lisette Melendez. And JMJ is run by Jam Master Jay, the DJ from Run DMC. He produced rap and R&B for bands including The Afros and Fam Lee.

The "majors" succumb to rap

Meanwhile the other record companies have fallen over themselves to emulate Def Jam's success. Atlantic has Atlantic Street and Capitol has its "Street Awareness Program". Walt Disney has launched two rap labels. One is The Hollywood Basic label, which caused a sensation when it released an album by the Lifer's Group, composed entirely of men serving life in New Jersey's Rahway Prison. The other, Hollywood, released a rap record by Prince Akeem which included the inflammatory words of Minister Louis D. Farrakhan. In six months the majors released more rap records than Def Jam did in six years.

While Public Enemy and NWA – Niggers With Attitude, famed for having their album *Efil4Zaggin* (Niggarz 4 Life in mirror-writing) banned in Great Britain – maintain the harsh political voice of rap, other bands are eager to compromise. Run-DMC's album, *Raising Hell,* the first rap album to make the top ten, included a song called "My Adidas". MC Hammer is sponsored by Pepsi and earns $40 million a year. In rap, everyone makes money. Simmons has used the money generated by rap to finance TV production a new wave of black films.

ABOVE: **NWA – Niggers With Attitude – have stirred up controversy on both sides of the Atlantic. They keep their** credibility as heroes of the streets by voicing black anger, while slick production ensures massive sales.

FOUR DECADES OF ESSENTIAL ALBUMS

THE FIFTIES

- *Golden Decade* – **Chuck Berry**
- *Bo Diddley* – **Bo Diddley**
- *The Sun Collection* – **Elvis Presley**
- *Legendary Masters* – **Fats Domino**
- *That'll Be the Day* – **Buddy Holly**
- *Original Greatest Hits* – **Jerry Lee Lewis**
- *Best of Muddy Waters* – **Muddy Waters**
- *Sam Cooke: The Man and His Music* – **Sam Cooke**
- *The Life and Times of Little Richard* – **Little Richard**
- *Rock Around the Clock* – **Bill Haley**

THE SIXTIES

- *A Man and His Soul* – **Ray Charles**
- *Pain in My Heart* – **Otis Redding**
- *The Temptations Sing Smokey* – **The Temptations**
- *Pet Sounds* – **The Beach Boys**
- *Sergeant Pepper's Lonely Hearts Club Band* – **The Beatles**
- *The Freewheelin' Bob Dylan* – **Bob Dylan**
- *The Doors* – **The Doors**
- *Are You Experienced?* – **Jimi Hendrix and the Experience**
- *In Dreams: The Greatest Hits* – **Roy Orbison**
- *Surrealistic Pillow* – **Jefferson Airplane**
- *Village Green Preservation Society* – **The Kinks**
- *Wheels of Fire* – **Cream**
- *Beggars' Banquet* – **The Rolling Stones**

THE SEVENTIES

- *Who's Next* – **The Who**
- *Dark Side of the Moon* – **Pink Floyd**
- *Young Americans* – **David Bowie**
- *Blue* – **Joni Mitchell**
- *After the Goldrush* – **Neil Young**
- *Exodus* – **Bob Marley**
- *Physical Graffiti* – **Led Zeppelin**
- *Imagine* – **John Lennon**
- *Transformer* – **Lou Reed**
- *A Night at the Opera* – **Queen**
- *Looking Back* – **Stevie Wonder**
- *Parallel Lines* – **Blondie**
- *Talking Heads 77* – **Talking Heads**
- *London Calling* – **The Clash**
- *C'est Chic* – **Chic**
- *Born to Run* – **Bruce Springsteen**

THE EIGHTIES

- *Like A Virgin* – **Madonna**
- *Regatta de Blanc* – **The Police**
- *Thriller* – **Michael Jackson**
- *Face Value* – **Phil Collins**
- *The Unforgettable Fire* – **U2**
- *Appetite for Destruction* – **Guns 'n' Roses**
- *The Message* – **Grandmaster Flash**
- *Raising Hell* – **Run DMC**
- *Murmur* – **REM**
- *The Cream of Eric Clapton* – **Eric Clapton**
- *Hatful of Hollow* – **The Smiths**

Page numbers in *italic* refer to picture captions.

A

A&M (label) 66–7
  PolyGram take-over 66, 92
  and Sex Pistols 101
Abaramson, Herb 21
Abbatiello, Sal 108
ABC (band) 102, *102*
ABC (label) 94
ABC-Paramount (label) 94
Ace, Johnny 10
Adler, Lou 28, 66
Afros, The 108
Aikman, Sir Alexander 59
"Ain't Got No Home" *19*
Aitken, Laurel 82
Ales, Barney 43
Allen, Rance 37
"Alley Oop" 66
Alpert, Herb 66, *66*
Amazing Rhythm Aces 14
Ambrose 48
America 61
American Federation of
  Musicians, recording ban 57
Ammons, Gene 17
Anderson, Laurie 78
Angel (label) 68
Animals, the 28, 54
Anna (label) 40
"Another Brick in the Wall" 88
Ant, Adam 88
Antilles (label) 85
Apple Corps Ltd. 62
Apple (label) 62–5
  Boutique 62
  headquarters *62*
  press office *64*
Arista (label) 27, 68, 72, 102
  and Clive Davis 75
Aristocrat 17
Armstrong, Louis 48, *49*, 70, 94
Art of Noise 102
Arthur Lewis Band 98
ASCAP 24–5
  royalties 24–5
Asher, Dick 88, 93
Ashford and Simpson 43
Ashley Famous agency 79
Asia 81, 102
Aspinall, Neil 62
Association, the 28
Asylum Records 82, 96
  and Geffen, Dave 79
  Warner Communications buy
    79
Atlantic Records 6, 13, 18, 21–
  3, 27, 28, 32, 35, 68, 75, 81,
  99
  Atco (label) 22, 28, 68, 78
  Atlantic Street (label) 108
  Cotillion (label) 68, 78
"Auf Wiedersehen" 50
Axton, Estelle 30–2
Axton, Packy 32
Ayers, Kevin 85
Azoff, Irving ("The Poison
  Dwarf") 6, 94, 96–7

B

Badarou, Wally 85
Badfinger 62
Baker, Anita 78
Baker, LaVern 21, *23*
Ballard, Florence 6, 43
Band, The 60
Barnett Samuel & Sons *48*
Basie, Count 28, 94
Bass, Fontella 18
Bay City Rollers 27
Baylor, Johnny 37
"Be-Bop-A-Lula" 60
Beach Boys 28, 54, *55*, 60
Beale Street 10
"Bear Cat" 10, *13*
Bearsville (label) 68
Beastie Boys 106, *106*
Beatles 6, 28, 35, 50, 53, *53*, 55,

62, 62–4, 72, 92, 102
  on Capitol 60
  Red and Blue albums 65
Bee Gees 68, *91*, 92
Beefheart, Captain 78, *78*
Belafonte, Harry *24*
Bell, Al 37
Bell (label) 27, 72
Belle Stars, the 86
Bennett, Tony 72
Benson, George 28
Berliner, Emile 24, 53, 90
Berliner, Jacob and Joseph 90
Berry, Chuck 8, *17*, 18, *18*, 28
Bertelsmann Music Group 27,
  56, 72
Big Red (label) 70
Big Tree (label) 68
Billboard magazine 21, 57, 61
Birdland 8
Birkin, Jane 91
"Birth of Cool" *57*, 59
Black, Bill 13
Black, Cilla 54
Black Fumes, The 108
Black Rock (CBS headquarters)
  6, 28
Blackwell, Chris 82–5, *82*
Bland, Bobby "Blue" 10
Blood, Sweat and Tears 72, 81
Blow, Kurtis 106
Blue Note (label) 55, 61, 68
"Blue Roses" 30, 32
Blue Sky (label) 68
"Blue Suede Shoes" 14, *14*
Bluebird (label) 68
Bluesway (label) 94
Bogart, Neil 92
"Boogie In My Bones" 82
Booker T. and the MGs 32, 34,
  34, 35
Boomtown Rats 88, 98
Boone, Pat *24*
Bowen, Jimmy 8
Bowie, David 27, 55, 98
Boy George 99, *99*
Boyd, Joe 85
Branson, Richard 6, 98, 99, *99*,
  101, *101*
"Breaks, The" 106
Brenston, Jackie 10, 17
Brilleaux, Lee 86
Bristol, Johnny 43
Brooks, Garth 61
Browne, Jackson 79, *79*, 81, 96
Cohen, Lyor 108
Brubeck, Dave 70
Brunswick Records 48, 54, 70,
  76, 94
Buffalo Springfield 22
Buggles 102
Burke, Solomon 22
Burnett, Chester "Howlin' Wolf"
  10, 17, 18
Burning Spear 85
Burns, George 92
Bylar, Fred 30
Byrds, the 28, 81

C

Cale, John 85
Campbell, Glen 60
Capitol Records 28, 54, 55, 57–
  61, 62, 68, 72, 104
  Capitol Tower (headquarters)
    6, 59

East Coast division 93
  "Street Awareness Program"
    (label) 108
Caribou (label) 68
Carnes, Kim 60
Carpenters, the 66
Cars, the 78
Casablanca (label) 92
Cash, Johnny 14
Cassidy, David 27
"Cathy's Clown" 76
"Cause I Love You" 32
CBS (Columbia Broadcasting
  System) 8, 28, 54, 55–6, 70–
  5, 81, 92, 99
  Black Rock headquarters 6,
    28
  Canada 88
  CBS/Columbia labels 68
  and Clive Davis 72–5, 93
  and DAT tape format 88
  and independent promoters
    88
  International 93
  LPs 70
  and Philips/Phonogram 90
  Records 75, 93, 106, 108
  Sony take-over 56, 75
  Stax Records deal with 37
  and Stiff Records 86
Chapman, Tracy 78
Charisma (label) 98
Charles, Ray 21, *21*, *30*, 32, *55*
Charly (label) 14
Checker (label) 13, 18, *19*
Chess, Leonard 17, 18
Chess, Marshall 18
Chess, Phil 17
Chess Records 6, 8, 10, 17–20,
  17, 28, 40, 94
Chic 22
Chicago 72, *72*
Christians, The 85
Chrysalis (label) 85
Chung, Mikey 85
City Lights (label) 68
Clapton, Eric 22
Clark, Petula 78
Clearpool Club 30
Cliff, Jimmy 85
Clooney, Rosemary 70
Coasters, the 22
Cochran, Eddie 28, 50
Cocker, Joe 54, *54*
Cole, Nat "King" 59
Cole, Natalie 60
Collins, Judy 79
Collins, Phil 99, *101*
Coltrane, John 22
Columbia 28, 48, 53, 70, *70*, 81,
  93, 104
  Black Rock headquarters 28
  and CBS 54, 75
  and Clive Davis 72–5
  and EMI 54
  International 54
  (Phonograph) Broadcasting
    System 70
  Pictures 27, 72
Command (label) 94
Como, Perry 27
compact discs 88, 104
Compass Point Allstars 85
Conley, Arthur 35

Cooder, Ry 78
Cope, Julian 85
copyright ownership 8
Coral (label) 94
Costello, Elvis 86, *86*
Cotillion (label) 68, 78
Cotton, Billy 48
Cotton, James 17
Count Basie 70
Cover Girls, The 108
"Cow Cow Boogie" 57
Crickets, the 94
Crosby, Bing *47*, 48, *49*, 94
Crosby, Stills and Nash *22*, 81
cross-over music 18, 22, 61
Crudup, Arthur "Big Boys" 13
Crystals, the 50
Cutting Crew 99

D

Damned, The 86, *86*
Dan, Steely 96
Darin, Bobby 6, 22, 50
Dark Horse (label) 68
Dave Clark Five 28, 54, *56*
Davis, Clive 27, 28, 72, 72–5,
  72, 93
Davis, Miles *57*, 59, 70, 83
Davis, Spencer *82*, 84
De La Soul 108
DeBerry, Jimmy 13
Decca 6, 8, 18, 28, 47–51, *47*,
  94
  and Brunswick Records *47*,
    70
  Dutch Decca 90
  London Records 50
  LPs 54
  radar *47*, 48
  UK 48, 50, 92, 94
  USA 48, 94
Def Jam (label) 6, 106–8
Def Leppard 93, *93*
Delicious Vinyl (label) 85
Dells, the 18
Delta Cats 17
Denny, Sandy 85
Denver, John 27
Derek and the Dominoes *90*
Desanto, Sugar Pie 18
Des'ree 104
Detroit Spinners 43
Deutsche Grammophon
  Gesellschaft 37, 54, *55*, 90
Dew Doo Man Records 108
Di Lello, Robert 64
Diamond, Neil 61, 72, 94, *94*
Diddley, Bo 18, *19*
Different Drummer (label) 68
Dixon, Willie 18
Dodd, Sir Coxone 82
Dollar 102
Dominoes, the 21, 40
Donegan, Lonnie 50
Donovan 72, *72*
Dorsey, Tommy 25
Dot Records *24*, 27, 28, 94
Double Fantasy 81
Downes, Geoffrey 102
Downtown Science 108
Dr Feelgood 86
Dr Hook 60
Drake, Nick 85
Drama 102

Draper, Simon 98, 99
Drifters, the 22
"Drinkin' Wine Spo-Dee-O-
  Dee" 21
Duck Rock 102
Duke (label) 10
Dunbar, Sly 85
Dunhill (label) 94
Duophone (label) 47
Duran Duran 55, *56*, 61
Dury, Ian 86
Dylan, Bob 28, 68, 72, 79, 81

E

Eagles, the 79, 81, 96
Eastman, John 64
Eastman, Lee 64
Eastman, Linda 64
Easton, Edward 53
Easton, Sheena 55, 60
Eckstine, Billy 17
Eddie & the Hot Rods 85
Eddy, Duane 50
Edison Bell Winner 48
Edmunds, Dave 86
Edwards, King 82
Efil4Zaggin 108
Electrola (label) 54, 90
Elektra (label) 81
  Warner Brothers buy 79
Elektra/Asylum (label) 68, 78,
  79–81
Elektra/Curb (label) 68
Ellington, Duke 25, 59, 70
Ellis, Terry 84
Emerson, Billy "the Kid" 13
Emerson Lake & Palmer *22*, 84
EMI 8, 28, 52–6, 54, 59, 62, 66,
  68, 92, 101
  Abbey Road studio 52
  and Apple (label) 62, 65
  CBS take-over bid 56
  and Columbia 70
  Lockwood, Joseph 53
  MCA agreement 94
  and Parlophone 53
  and Stiff Records 86
  USA 60, 61, 68
Emotions, the 37
Ensign (label) 98
Enterprise Records 37
Epic (label) 68
EPMD 108
Epstein, Brian 53, 62
Eric B. & Rakim 108
Ertegun, Ahmet 21, *21*, 81, 99
Ertegun, Neshui 22
Esther, Little 21
Eurythmics 27
Everly Brothers 50, *50*, 76
Exorcist, The (film) 99

F

Face Dances 88
Fairport Convention 85, 98
Faith, Percy 70
Fam Lee 108
Fame, Georgie 54
Fame Records 32
  Studios 22
Fever Records 108
Fields, Gracie 50
Fifth Dimension 81
Flack, Roberta 22
Flamingos, the 18
Fleetwood Mac 78
Floyd, Eddie *30*, 35
Forbes "Four Hundred" 79
Ford, Mary 59
Ford, Tennessee Ernie 61
Four Tops *41*, 43
Fourth & Broadway (label) 85
Frampton, Peter 92
Frankie Goes to Hollywood 85,
  102, *102*
Franklin, Aretha 28, 72, 75
Free 84

Freed, Alan 8, 18, 88
Fresh Prince 108
Friedkin, William 99
Frontline, management co. 96
Fulson, Lowell 18
Fuqua, Henry 41, 43
Fury, Billy 28, 50, *50*

G

Gabriel, Peter 81
Gainsbourg, Serge 91
Gambino family (Mafia) 88
Garner, Erroll 21, *22*
Gaye, Marvin 41, 43
Geffen, Dave 79–81, 96
Geffen (label) 79, 81, 97
Geldof, Bob 88, 98
General Electric 24
General Recording Tape 18, 68
Gentry, Bobby 60
Gerry and the Pacemakers 28, *70*
Gershwin, George 76
"Get a Job" 40
Getz, Stan 17
"Ghee Whiz" 32, *33*
Gillespie, Dizzy 25, *26*
"Gimme Some Lovin'" 84
Glitter, Gary 27
Goodman, Benny 25, 59, 70
Gordon, Rosco 10
Gordy, Berry 28, 38–45, *38*
Gortikov, Stan 60
"Got a Job" 40
Gotti, John 104
Gramophone Company of India 60
Gramophone Company, The 53
Grand Funk Railroad 60
Grape, Moby 28
Grease 92
"Great Pretender, The" 91
Great Rock 'n' Roll Swindle, The (film) 98
Great White 61
"Green Onions" *34*
Grimes, Tiny 21
Grossman, Albert 28
Grunt (label) 68
Guns "N" Roses 81
Guy, Buddy 18, *21*

H

Haley, Bill 10, 94
Hall & Oates 27
Hammond, John 28
Harder They Come, The (film) 85
Harris, Emmylou 78
Harrison, George 64, *65*
Harvest (label) 68
Hawkins, Dale 18
Hayes, Isaac 34, *36*, 37
Hayward, Lance 82, 83
Heaven 17: 99
Hendrix, Jimi 28
Henley, Don 96, *96*
Henry, Clarence "Frogman" 18, *19*
Herman, Woody 17
Herman's Hermits 28
"Hey Jude" 62
Hi-Tension 85
Hill and Range 27
"hippie heaven" festival 28
HMV (label) 53–4
  Nipper the dog 25, 53–4, *55*, 90, *90*
Holiday, Billie 28
Holland-Dozier-Holland 43, 45
Hollies, the 28, 54
Holly, Buddy 94
Hollywood Argyles 66
Hollywood Basic (label) 108
Hollywood (label) 108
Holzman, Jac 79, 81
Hooker, Earl 10

Hopkin, Mary 62, *64*
Horn, Trevor 102
Horton, Walter 10
Hot Buttered Soul 37
Houston, Whitney 27, 72, 88
Human League 99
Humperdinck, Engelbert 51
Hunter, Tab 76
Husky, Ferlin 61
Hylton, Jack 48

I

"I Just Want to Make Love to You" 18
"I Walk the Line" 14
Ian Dury and the Blockheads 102
"If Loving You is Wrong" 37
Ifield, Frank 54
"I'll Be Satisfied" 40
"I'm A Man" 84
Imperial (label) 48, 55, 59, 61
Impulse (label) 94
"In the Midnight Hour" 21
independent promoters 88
Ingram, Luther 37
Inner Circle 85
Ionnucci, Sal 60
Iron Butterfly 22
Isgro, Joe 104
Island Records 68, 82–5, *82*, 99, 102
  Compass Point studio 85
  logo *82*
  and movies 85
  Notting Hill studio 85
  PolyGram buy 92
  and Stiff Records 86
Isley Brothers 43, 45, *45*

J

Jackson Five 43, *43*, 45
Jackson, Michael 48, *70*, 75, 88
Jakeman, Andrew "Jake" 86
James, Elmore 17
James, Etta 18
James, Sonny 61
Janus (label) 18
Japan 99
Jazz Singer, The 61
Jazzy Jeff 108
"Je T'aime" 91
Jet Kirschner (label) 68
JMJ (Jam Master Jay) (label) 108
Joel, Billy 72
John, Elton 81, *81*, 94
John, Robert 60
Johnson, Holly 102, *102*
Johnson, Marv 40
Jolson, Al 25, 48
Jones, Booker T. 32, 34, 37
Jones, Grace 85, 102
Jones, Tom 51
Joplin, Janis 28, 72, *72*
Jotis Records *35*
Jovi, Bon 93, *93*
juke box 8

K

Kassner, Eddie 6
"Keep on Running" 84
Keep Your Eyes on Me 66
Keita, Salif 85
Kenton, Stan 59
Kern, Jerome 76
King, B.B. 10, *11*
King, Carole 66
King Crimson 84
Kings of Rhythm 10, 17
Kinks, the 72, 78
Kiss of the Spiderwoman (film) 85
Klein, Alan 6, 64
Knack, the 60
Knapp, Jack 48
Knight, Frederick 37

Knight, Gladys (and the Pips) 43, 45, *45*
Knight, Jean 37
"Knock on Wood" *30*
Knox, Buddy 8
Kramer, Billy J. and the Dakotas 28, 54, *55*

L

Led Zeppelin 22
Ledbetter, Hubbie "Leadbelly" 50
Lee, Julia 59
Lee, Peggy 59, 94
"Legalize It" 98
Leiber, Jerry 22, 27
Lennon, John 62, 64, 65, *65*, 102
  assassination of 81
"Let It Be" *62*
Levy, Morris 6, 8, 13, 104
Lewis, Jerry Lee 10, *11*, 14, *14*
Lewis, Sir Edward 47–8, 50, 51
Liberty (label) 28, 55, 57, 61
Life-song (label) 68
Lifer's Group 108
"Lille Marlene" 54
Lindo, Blanche 83
Lippman, Michael 96
"Little Red Rooster" 18
"Little Sheila" 82
Liverpool '86 102
Livingston, Alan 60
LL Cool J 106, *106*, 108
Loc, Tone 85
Lockwood, Sir Joseph 53, 54, 60
Lomax, Jackie 62
Lombardo, Guy 48, 59
London Records 50
"Lonely Bull" 66
"Lonely Teardrops" 40
Lopez, Trini 78
Loverboy 88
Lovich, Lena 86
Lowe, Nick 86, *86*
LP systems 27, *27*, 54
"Lullaby of Birdland" 8
Lundvall, Bruce 61
Lutcher, Nellie 59
Lydon, John 98
Lymon, Frankie 8
Lynn, Vera 50, *50*

M

McLaren, Malcolm 98, 101, 102
McCartney, Paul 56, 61, 62, 64, 98
McGhee, Brownie 79
McGhee, Stick 21
McKay, Barry 6
McKenzie, Scott 28
McPhatter, Clyde 21, 40
Madison (label) 66
Madness 86
Madonna 78
Magazine 99
Manfred Mann 54
Mango (label) 85
Manhattan (label) 56, 61
Manhattan Transfer 22
Manilow, Barry 27, 72
Manor recording studio, The 98, 99
Marconi Company 24
Maria, Teena 45
Marley, Bob and the Wailers 84, 85
Marshall, Paul 88
Martha and the Vandellas 41, *43*
Martin Dean 59, 78
Martin, George 53, *53*
Martyn, John 85
Marvelettes, the *39*, 41, 43
Matadors 40
Mathis, Johnny 70
May, Billy 59

"Maybellene" 8, 18
MC Hammer 61, 104, 108
MCA (label) 6, 45, 50, 68, 94–7
  and Irving Azoff 96, 97
  re-issues 18
Mel and Tim 37
Melendez, Lisette 108
Melvin, Harold and the Blue Notes 75
Members, the 99
Memphis Recording Service 10, 13
Menon, Bhaskar 60
Mercer, Johnny 57, 59
Mercury (label) 32, 59, 91
MGM (label) 91
Mic Tee Lux 108
Midler, Bette 22
Miller, Glen 25, *27*
Miller, Mitch 70, 91
Miller, Steve 28
Millie 84
Mills Brothers 48
Milton, Little 18
Mingus, Charles 22
Miracles *see* Matadors
Mitchell, Guy 70
Mitchell, Joni 78, *78*, 79, *79*, 81
Mocambo tavern, The 17
Modern Jazz Quartet 22, *23*, 62
Modern (label) 10
"Money" 40
Monk, Thelonious 70
Monotones, the 18
Monterey Pop Festival 28, 72
Moody Blues 51
Moore, Samuel *see* Sam and Dave
Moore, Scotty 13
Morse, Ella Mae 57, 61
Moss, Jerry 66
Motels, the 61
Motorhead 86
Motown (label) 6, 38–46, *38*, *39*, 68, 97, *97*
  Artist's Development Department 40, *43*
  Britain, 1965 tour of *41*
  company roster 43
  MCA deal with 45
  unpaid royalties 45
Mott the Hoople 84
Move, the 54
"My Adidas" 108
"My Boy Lollipop" 82
"My Happiness" 13
"My Sharona" 60

N

Naked Truth 104
Nash, Johnny 85
Ned's Atomic Dustbin 104
Nelson, Ricky 50, 94
Nemperor (label) 68
"Network" *see* independent promoters
Newkirk 108
Newman, Tom 98, 99
Newton-John, Olivia 94, *94*
Nicks, Stevie 96
Nikki D 108
Nipper the dog *see* HMV
"No Future" 98
Nonesuch (label) 68
North American Phonograph 53
NWA (Niggers With Attitude) 108, *108*
Nyro, Laura 28, 81

O

OBR (Original Black Records) (label) 108
Ochs, Phil 66, 79
Ode Records 28
O'Jays, The 75
Old Town (label) 8
Oldfield, Mike 98, 99

Ono, Yoko 65, *65*
Orbison, Roy 14, 50, *50*
Original Dixieland Jazz Band *24, 25*

P

Paisley Park (label) 78
Paley, William 75
Palmer, Robert 85
Paramount 37, 94
Paramount Pictures Music Division 35
Parker, Charlie 8
Parker, "Colonel" Tom 13, 27
Parker, Graham 86
Parker, Junior 10
Parlophone (label) 28, 53, 54, 62
  labels *53*
Parnes, Larry *50*
Parton, Dolly 27
Paul, Billy 75
Paul, Les 59
Payne, Silas 10
payola 104
  scandal 8, 88
Penetration 99
Perkins, Carl 14
Perry, Lee 85
Pet Shop Boys, the 55
Peter and Gordon 54
Peter, Paul and Mary 76
Petty, Tom 6
Phaedra 98
Philadelphia International (label) 68, 75
Philips 54, 91, 92
  CD technology 88
  label 84
  optical disc 92
  and Phonogram 90
  and Sony, CD factory 92
Philles (label) 28
Phillips, Dewey 13
Phillips, Sam 8, 10, *10*, 13, 14, 27, 32
Phonogram (label) 90, 91
Pickett, Wilson 21, *23*
Pine, Courtney 85
Pink Cadillac 14
Pink Floyd 55, 61, 88, 98
Plastic Ono Band 62
Platters, the 91, *91*
Please Hammer Don't Hurt 'Em 61
"Please Mister Postman" 41
Pointer Sisters 94
Polydor (label) 8
  HMV trade mark 90
Polydor/Phonogram (labels) merge 91
PolyGram (label) 51, 68, 88, 90–2, 92, 93, 104
  and WEA 78
Poole, Brian and the Tremeloes 28, 50
Pop, Iggy 86
Porter, Cole 76
Porter, David 34
Portrait (label) 68
"Power of Love, The" 102
Prater, David *see* Sam and Dave
Presley, Elvis 8, 10, 13, *13*, 27, *27*, 28, 30, 32, 54, 72, 102
Preston, Billy 62
Prince 78
Prince Akeem 108
Prince Paul 108
Prine, John 14
Prisonaires, the 13
Procul Harum 66, *67*
Profile Records 108
Propaganda 102
Pryor, Richard 37
Public Enemy 106, 108
Public Image Ltd. 98

INDEX

Q

Queen 55, 61
Quicksilver Messenger Service 28
Quintessence 84

R

Radar Records 86
"Rage Hard" 102
Raising Hell 108
RAL (Rush Associated Labels) 108
Ramones, the 68, 86
"Rapper's Delight" 106
Rare Earth (band) 43
Rare Earth Records 43
Rascals, the 22
RCA (label) 24–7, 28, 51, 54, 55, 56, 68, 72
RCA Victor 8, 13, *24*, 54
Read, Mike 102
Record Industry Association of America 43
Redding, Otis 22, *30*, 35, *35*
"Reefer Song, The" *26*
"Reet Petite" *38*, 40
Reeves, Martha 43, 45, 97, *97*
Regal Zonophone 54
Reid, Duke 82
"Relax" 102
Reprise (label) 76, 78
Resident Alien 108
Revere, Paul and the Raiders 28
"Revolution" 62, *65*
Rex (label) 48
Reynolds, Barry 85
Rhythm and blues 8, 10, 17, 21, 32
British bands *48*
labels 28
Rich, Charlie 14
Richard, Cliff 28, *53*, 54, 60
and the Shadows 53
Richard, Little 6, 50
Richards, Keith 6
Richie, Lionel 97, *97*
Riddle, Nelson 59
Riley, Billy Lee 14
Roberts, Eliot 81
Robinson, David 6, 86
Robinson, Smokey 40, 41, *41*, 43
and the Miracles 41, *41*
"Rock Island Line" 50
rock-and-roll 8, 10, 17, 18, 28, 50, 60
"Rocket 88" 10, 17
Rocket (label) 68
Rodgers, Richard 76
Rogers, Kenny 78
Rolling Stones 6, 18, 22, 28, 32, 50, 51, *51*, 56, 68, 98
Records 68
Ronettes, the 50
Ronstadt, Linda 60, *61*, 79, *79*, 81
Ropin' The Wind 61
Rosco, Gordon 17
Ross, Diana 40, 43, 45
Ross, Isaiah "Dr" 13
Roulette Records 6, 8
Roxy Music 85, *85*
Roy and Millie 82
Royal Spades 32
royalties 6, 8
RPM (label) 10
RSO (label) 92
Rubin, Rick 106
Ruffin, Jimmy 43
Run DMC 106, 108
Rush 93
Rush Artist Management 106
Rush, Otis 18
Rush, Tom 28

S

Sabit, Dr 21

Sam and Dave 22, 34, 35, *35*
"San Francisco (Be Sure to Wear Some Flowers in Your Hair)" 28
Santana 72
Satellite Records 32
Saturday Night Fever 68, 92
Scaffold 98
Scaggs, Boz 96
"Scarlet Ribbons" *24*
Scorpions 93
Seal 102
Seekers, the 54
Segelstein, Irwin 75
Seger, Bob 61
Sellers, Peter 53
Seraphim (label) 68
Sergeant Pepper's Lonely Hearts Club Band 35
(film) 92, *92*
Sex Pistols 68, 98, 99
A&M signing of 66, *67*, 101
Virgin signing of 101, *101*
"Shake, Rattle and Roll" 22
Shakespeare, Robbie 85
Shannon, Del 50
"She loves You" *53*
"Shop Around" 41
Shore, Dinah 27
Siemens 90, 91, 92
Silhouettes 40
Sill, Lester 28
Simmons, Russell "Rush" 106, 108
Simon and Garfunkel 28
Simple Minds 99
Sinatra, Frank 25, 59, *59*
and Reprise 76
Sinatra, Nancy 78
Singleton, Shelby 14
Sire (label) 68, 78
Sister Sledge 22
Skids, the 99
Slack, Freddie 57
"Slave to the Rhythm" 102
Sledge, Percy 22
Slick Rick 108
Sly and Robbie 85
Smith, Bessie 70
Smith, Carl 14, *14*
Smith, Joe 81
Sony 56, 75, *75*, 104
CDs 88
DAT tape format 88
Music 108
Soho Square (label) 104
Soul Children, the 37
Source (label) 68
South, Joe 60
Sparks 85
Speakeasy Club *28*
Speciality (label) 13, 28
Spector, Phil 28
Spencer Davis Group 84, 91
Spooky Tooth 84
Springfield, Dusty 91
Springfield, Rick 27
Springsteen, Bruce 28, 72, 75, *75*
SSS International (label) 14
Staples, the *36*, 37
Starr, Ringo 64
"Stars and Stripes" *24*
Stax Records 6, *13*, 28, 30–7
and CBS 37, 75
Partee subsidiary 37
Soulsville U.S.A. 22, 30
Wattstax charity concert 37
Steele, Tommy 50
Stein, Jules 94
Sterling, Louis 54
Stetsatonic 108
Steve Miller Band 60
Stevens, Cat 66, *66*, 84
Stewart, Jim 30–7
Stiff Records 6, 86–7
Stigwood, Robert 92
Stills, Steven 81

Stoller, Mike 22, 27
Stone, Cliffie 61
"Stone Crazy" *21*
Streisand, Barbara 81
Strong, Barrett 40
Student, The magazine 98
Sugarhill Gang 106
Summer, Donna 81, *81*, 92
Sun Records 8, *10*, 13–14, 27, 28, 32
Studios 6, 10, 14
Supremes 6, *41*, 43, *45*
Swan (label) *53*
Swan Song (label) 68
Sweet, 27

T

Tabu (label) 68
Talking Heads 78
Tamla Motown *see* Motown
Tammy 40
Tangerine Dream 98
Tashjian, Valerie 104
Tashran 108
Taste of Honey, A 60
Tatum, Art 59
Taylor, James 62, 78
Taylor, Johnnie 37
Taylor, Koko 18
Teller, Al 97
"Telstar" 50
Temple, Radha Krishna 62
Temptations *41*, 43, 45, *45*
10 CC 98
Terry, Sonny 79
Tex, Joe 22
That Nigger's Crazy 37
"That's All Right, Mama" 13
"These Arms of Mine" *30*
Third Bass 108
Third World 85
"This Guy's in Love With You" 66
Thomas, Carla 32, *33*, 35
Thomas, Rufus 10, *13*, 32, *33*, 37
Thompson, Hank 61
Thompson, Richard and Linda 85
Thompson, Sticky 85
Thorn Electrical Industries 55
Three Dog Night 81
Tiffany 97
Tijuana Brass 66
Tin Pan Alley *7*
Tisch, Larry 75
Tje, Hein 91
Toots and the Maytals 85, *85*
Tornados, the 50
Tosh, Peter 98
Traffic 84
Travis, Randy 78
Trip to the Bountiful, The (film) 85
Tripoli, Andy "Panda" 108
Troy, Doris 62
Tubes, The 61, *61*
Tubular Bells 98, 99, *99*
Tull, Jethro 84
Turner, Big Joe 21, *22*
Turner, Ike 10, 17, 50
Turner, Tina 50, 61
"Twinkle Star" 66
"Two Tribes" 102

U

U-2 85
United Artists Records 55, 61, 68, 91
Unlimited Gold (label) 68

V

V (label) *26*
Van Halen 78
van Zoelen, Hans 90
Vee Jay Records *36*, 60
Verve (label) 91

Victor (label) 24–5, *24*, 25
Victor Talking Machine Company 24
"Video Killed the Radio Star" 102
Vincent, Gene 28, *57*, *59*, 60
Virgin Records 85, 99
logo *99*
Vocalion (label) 48

W

Waits, Tom 81, *81*
Wakely, Jimmy 61
Wakeman, Rick 66
Walker Brothers 92
Walker, Junior 43
Wall 88
Waller, Fats 25, *26*
Wallichs, Clive 57
Wallichs, Glenn 57, 59–60
Walter, Little 18
Warner
Brothers 28, 35, 75, 76–8, 81, 104
Communications 22, 79, 92, 93
Warner-PolyGram merger 93
WEA (Warner Elektra Atlantic) 22, 55, 68, 78
and Irving Azoff 97
Warner Records 68, 88
Warner-Curb (label) 68
Warner-Spector (label) 68
Warwick, Dionne 72
Was Not Was 81
Waters
Muddy 17, *17*, 18
"Way Over There" 41
"Wee Wee Hours" 18
Weiss, Hy 8
Welcome to the Pleasure Dome 102
"We'll Meet" 82
Wells, Mary 41, 43
Westminster (label) 94
Weston Electric 54
Weston, Kim 43
Weston, Paul 70
Wexler, Jerry 21, 22, 32, 81

Wham! 6
"What'd I Say" 32
"White Christmas" 48, *48*
"Whiter Shade of Pale, A" *67*
Whitesnake 81
Who, The 6, 68, 88, 94, 98
Whodini 108
"Whole Lotta Shakin' Goin' On" 14
"Who's Making Love?" 37
"Why Do Fools Fall in Love?" 8
Wild Romance 66
"Wild Thing" 85
William Morris agency 79
Williams, Alyson 108
Williams, Andy 72
Williams, Hank 78
Williamson, Sonny Boy 18
Willis, Chuck 21
Wilson, Jacki *94*
Wilson, Jackie 38, *38*
Wilson, Paul 45
Wingsong (label) 68
Winter, Johnny and Edgar 72
Winwood, Muff 84, 104
Winwood, Steve 84
Witchseason Productions 85
WLAC (Nashville) 10
WLAY (Muscle Shoals) 10
Wonder, Stevie *41*, 43, 45, *47*, 97, *97*
"World Shut Your Mouth" 85
WRAC (Memphis) 10
Wreckless Eric 86
Wright, Chris 84

Y

Yachts, the 86
Yardbirds, the 28, 54
"Yellow Rose of Texas, The" 8
Yes 22, 102
Yetnikoff, Walter 6, 75, 88, 93, 94
"You Better You Bet" 88
"You Got What It Takes" 40
Young, Neil 78, 81

Z

Zavaroni, Lena 37
ZTT (label) 85, 102–3

PICTURE CREDITS

T = top; B = bottom; L = left; R = right; M = middle

The great majority of the pictures in this book were provided by **Pictorial Press.** The exceptions are listed below and are reproduced courtesy of:

The Apple Corps Ltd: 62, 65T.

Adrian Boot: 72–3, 82R, 83.

The Decca Record Company: 47 (three), 48BL, 49BR.

Tommy Hanley: 63, 64 (two), 65B.

Rock On: 10, p17 (two), 21TR, 21BR, 23T, 24L & TL, 25BR, 30 (two), 32BR, 38R, 39TR & BR, 40T, 44T, 48T, 54MR, 57, 70B, 76, 82TL & B, 94.

Sony UK Ltd: 75

(Uncredited record sleeves were provided by Mirco De Cet.)